Reviews of *Smartwoman*

'*Smartwoman* is a compelling, informative, empowering and provocative must-read that provides practical tools, tips, guidelines and advice so that we, as women, can better control our financial destiny. It is forthright, honest and compassionate, and explains how we can take charge of our hard-earned money and build a purposeful relationship with it. It challenges us to better understand the value of money, how we save and spend it, how we protect and preserve it, and how we align this with our sense of purpose by setting smart goals.' — **Professor Shirley Zinn**

'Though the book is called *Smartwoman*, it is relevant to both men and women. Understanding your finances, your money personality and your relationship with money is relevant at any age. The book shares nuggets of wisdom at different milestones of one's life, whether it's the four pillars of life, the seven steps of building your designer life, or just implications of each phase and scenarios in our life journey. Practical tools shared in the book make it a valuable handbook for a holistic life of purpose. For me, being happy comes from within, being comfortable in your own skin, embracing your strengths and your weaknesses.

'However, wealth enables you to design your desired life; whether it's a life of giving, investing, indulgence, or all of the above, it is a choice each one of us makes as we try to live a life of purpose.

'I will definitely get a few copies for my nieces and nephews as a handbook for creating and maintaining wealth and a balanced life.'
— **Dr Judy Dlamini, Executive Chairman, Mbekani Group**

smart woman

How to gain financial independence *and* create wealth

SYLVIA WALKER

Smartwoman
Published by Zebra Press
an imprint of Penguin Random House South Africa (Pty) Ltd
Reg. No. 1953/000441/07
The Estuaries No. 4, Oxbow Crescent, Century Avenue, Century City, 7441
PO Box 1144, Cape Town, 8000, South Africa
www.penguinbooks.co.za

First edition 2017
Second edition 2022
Reprinted in 2025

3 5 7 9 10 8 6 4 2

Publication © Zebra Press 2022
Text © Sylvia Walker 2022

Cover illustration: iStockphoto

All rights reserved. No part of this publication may be reproduced,
stored in a retrieval system or transmitted, in any form or by any means,
electronic, mechanical, photocopying, recording or otherwise,
without the prior written permission of the copyright owners.

PUBLISHER: Marlene Fryer
MANAGING EDITOR: Ronel Richter-Herbert
EDITOR: Christa Büttner-Rohwer
PROOFREADER: Lauren Smith
COVER DESIGNER: Sean Robertson/Ryan Africa
TEXT DESIGNER: Ryan Africa
TYPESETTER: Ryan Africa

Set in 11.5 pt on 15.5 pt Adobe Garamond

Printed by novus print, a division of Novus Holdings

ISBN 978 1 77609 641 1 (print)
ISBN 978 1 77609 642 8 (ePub)

Disclaimer

This book provides general information about money and investment, and every effort has been made to ensure that the contents of the book are accurate at the time of publication. Investment markets and the factors that drive them are constantly changing, however. Information in this book is in no way intended to replace or supersede independent or other professional advice. Neither the author nor the publisher may be held responsible for any action or claim resulting from the use of this book or any information contained in it.

Contents

Foreword ix
Acknowledgements xi
Preface xiii

Chapter 1   Why a book for women? 1
Chapter 2   The magic of money 7
Chapter 3   Smart thoughts lead to success 13
Chapter 4   Your money personality 21
Chapter 5   Whose life is it anyway? 29
Chapter 6   Creating your designer life 43
Chapter 7   Money and marriage 55
Chapter 8   The devastation of divorce 67
Chapter 9   Take control 75
Chapter 10   Dealing with debt 87
Chapter 11   Getting your hustle on 95
Chapter 12   Setting smart goals 101
Chapter 13   Retire rich 111
Chapter 14   Fast money, burnt fingers 123
Chapter 15   How much are you worth? 129
Chapter 16   Is your home your nest egg? 135
Chapter 17   Investing: Understanding the basics 141
Chapter 18   Investment risk and you 153
Chapter 19   The financial markets made simple 161
Chapter 20   Investing in equities 173
Chapter 21   Investing in property 183
Chapter 22   Investing through financial services companies 193
Chapter 23   Advice: Man or machine? 201

Chapter 24 Kruger to crypto – alternative investments 211
Chapter 25 Protecting your wealth when life throws
            you off course 217
Chapter 26 The show must go on 225
Chapter 27 Get smart, get going and get rich 231

Appendix 1 235
Appendix 2 236
Appendix 3 237
Appendix 4 238
Appendix 5 240

References 243

For Derek and Andrea, my reasons for being.

Foreword

A male editor of mine once asked me why I was writing an article about 'women and money'. 'Surely money is gender neutral,' he argued. It is a valid question, and I understand why men struggle to see the point of finance books specifically written for women.

Yet the reality is that money is different for women. Obviously not the actual notes and coins, but more around how we engage with money and the role it plays in a woman's life.

Possibly because of years of living in patriarchal societies where men went to work and took care of the family finances, many women lack confidence when it comes to managing their own finances. A financial adviser told me recently that she believes it is because many girls at school grow up with a fear of maths. I investigated this, and it is a real thing. For some reason girls are more likely to suffer from 'maths anxiety' than boys. There is a lot of research explaining why, but the key takeaway is that even though your personal finances have nothing to do with your mathematical ability, it sets up a mindset that if it has to do with numbers, 'I can't do it.'

The irony is that women, more than men, need to be taking control of their finances.

Just consider these alarming statistics: salary surveys show women on average earn 30% less than men. Executive pay comparisons show that women earn 28% less than men for the same job! The PWC Women in Work Index shows that even in developed countries, women earn on average 16% less than men. So, it's no wonder that we sometimes wish a man could come along and save us financially.

Yet the adage of a 'man is a financial plan' is a very dangerous strategy! Whether we want it or not, 80% of us will manage our own money during our lifetime – because we remain single, divorce or are widowed. So, opting out is not an option.

The Old Mutual Savings and Investment Monitor survey, which only interviews working, urban mothers, found that around half of them were raising children on their own and only around a quarter received regular income from the father.

The PWC survey found that in the 37 most developed economies in the world, women undertake 75% of childcare responsibilities – and that is in developed countries!

Around 50% of marriages in South Africa end in divorce, and studies in the US estimate that a woman's standard of living drops by around a quarter, while a man's actually increases. This is usually because her career has taken a backseat while she raises her children.

And even if you have the perfect marriage and never divorce, statistically your husband is more likely to die before you. Statistics show that you will outlive your partner by seven years. This is not a subject we like to talk about, but we cannot shy away from it, as we need to ensure that we are financially prepared for this reality.

These are the reasons why financial books for women are so important. Especially one like *Smartwoman*, which explains money in such an easily accessible way. By the time you have finished reading this book, you will realise that you do not have to be a maths expert to understand how to manage a budget or start an investment!

And the most important message I would love to get across is that *women* are the ones who should be managing the family's finances. Our nurturing side and concern for our family's future often make us better decision-makers. We are less likely to take uncalculated risks, and we ask a lot of questions before making a commitment. We focus on goal outcomes rather than 'beating the market'.

On a personal level, learning how to manage your money, making smart money decisions and identifying your money triggers will enrich your life – not only financially, but emotionally. Be a Smartwoman, read this book and start your journey towards financial confidence!

MAYA FISHER-FRENCH
MAYA ON MONEY

Acknowledgements

The English poet John Donne wrote that 'No man is an island', and no task such as this one can be completed without the help of other people. Some were directly involved; others formed part of the tapestry without knowing it – their situations and stories are woven in to illustrate certain points.

Speaking of illustrating points – one can't write a book about money without some numbers. I have tried to keep these to a minimum, as endless graphs and figures can be daunting. I needed some figures, though, to illuminate particular points along the way.

When it came to information about returns of the JSE All Share Index and a resultant graph, Etienne Venter, retail business analyst manager at Prudential Asset Managers, didn't hesitate to assist when I asked for help. Stephen Walker, actuary at Old Mutual, provided me with statistics on life expectancy and taught me something new about how this is calculated.

Examining and understanding asset class returns is critical when making investment decisions, and Maxwell Mojapelo, investment analyst from Sanlam Investments, kindly provided me with various tables and helped clarify issues around this.

No book of this nature would be complete without a money personality assessment, so I scoured the internet for one that was easy to do and accurate in its assessment. Liz Koh, author and certified financial planner from Moneymax in New Zealand, generously allowed me to include her excellent assessment.

Peter Stefan and Taryn Hirsch, senior policy advisers at ASISA, provided information and assistance around some of the issues with which investors grapple.

Property is always a fascinating area of investment, and Kobus Lamprecht, head of research and publications at Rode and Associates, shed light on this area by providing valuable information on the South African property index.

Last, but not least, Derek Walker CA (SA), provided numerous calculations to illustrate different points in the book.

My part in this was doing the research and writing. There is a whole team of people who take my words and get them onto a bookshelf or into a downloadable format. Some I know, as I work directly with them, others I never get to see or meet. So, thanks to Christa Büttner-Rohwer for editing, Ronel Richter-Herbert for project-managing, and the rest of the team at Penguin Random House South Africa who were part of this process.

Finally, a special thanks to Maya Fisher-French for writing the Foreword, as well as Dr Judy Dlamini and Professor Shirley Zinn for taking the time to read and review the book.

Preface

Most people tend not to spend much time dwelling on money: we have lives to live and experiences to enjoy. Yet we cannot ignore the importance of money in our lives, particularly as women.

This issue has always been close to my heart. As a marketing manager for a blue-chip financial services company, I was fortunate to spend considerable time focusing on women and their finances, which was a great fit between my personal and professional beliefs.

After I left the corporate world at the end of 2014, I seriously considered writing a book about finances – a South African book, written by a woman, for women.

Over the years, I'd worked on and off on various chapters of an untitled book, covering different aspects of life that affect women and some of the financial implications. As my life evolved both personally and professionally, I added chapters that reflected on various situations I had observed. It's very interesting for me to look back and read through some of that work – it was almost like a diary of sorts, without me consciously realising it at the time.

Running through it all, of course, was money, as it does for any woman. No matter where life takes us or which situations we find ourselves in, money always hovers silently in the background. It can facilitate, empower and manipulate. We may often wish that we had more, and there may even be rare times when we wish we had less. But it is always there, part of life.

Somewhere along the way, the Smartwoman concept was born: the woman who learns from her mistakes, knows what to do at all times and generally makes the right decisions. She is the smart one – the one we all admire. Yet she is inside all of us. Sometimes it just takes a bit of coaxing and encouragement to get her to show her face.

I had written a few other non-fiction books before tackling this one, but *Smartwoman* had always been on my bucket list. When I finally sat down to draft a proposal, the book took on a fresh new approach and purpose. The world had changed over the years, and on a personal and professional level I had learnt so much and grown in so many areas. Smartwoman was going to focus on financial freedom (that elusive thing we all strive for) and growing wealth. The Smartwoman is still wise, makes the right decisions with her money and knows what to do to get rich!

So, in roughly three months, working flat out, I wrote the book from scratch. What about all the thousands of words I had written over the previous years? They have been mothballed – maybe to be resuscitated at some point, or maybe not.

So, why a book for women? The world of money and finances is still very male-dominated, although some strides have been made in recent years. There is also a language spoken in this world that only people in the industry understand. This jargon, along with an (often unintentional) male perspective, may leave many women feeling patronised and excluded.

It should be the opposite. Women are a major driving force in the economy and opportunities are endless. With so many women earning really good money comes the responsibility of managing it effectively. Many women earn the lion's share of income in the household, and in many other cases, women are single parents.

It is not just at times of crisis, such as divorce or widowhood, that a woman needs to take care of finances – it should be part of her lifestyle from her first working day.

The same principles are true for men, and this book is just as relevant for the male reader. Despite the fact that we presume that men are more clued up when it comes to managing money, I have often seen the opposite. So, men should also be able to benefit from following in the Smartwoman's footsteps!

I had fun writing this book. I learnt some new things – I am a knowledge junkie – and was able to see certain situations in a different light,

PREFACE

being outside of the big corporate financial world. Distance does provide objectivity!

My aim with *Smartwoman* was to create an understanding of money in our lives, how to be smart with it, and how to best use it to live happy and fulfilled lives, both today and tomorrow.

I hope you find it useful and enjoy reading it as much as I enjoyed writing it.

SYLVIA WALKER
CAPE TOWN
OCTOBER 2021

Chapter 1

Why a book for women?

> 'I truly believe that women should be financially independent from their men. And let's face it, money gives men the power to run the show. It gives men the power to define value. They define what's sexy. And men define what's feminine. It's ridiculous.'
>
> – *Beyoncé*

Getting rich isn't easy. If it were, many more people would have managed it by now. But have you ever wondered why some people seem to have so much money and others just seem to scrape by from payday to payday? What do smart people seem to know, and do, that is different from other people? These are fundamental questions when you look at building your wealth.

It all starts with money. Without money you can't live and you can't even think about building wealth. And there are only two things you can do with money – spend it or save it.

Life is all about choices, and smart choices build wealth. Money makes money, so with the right mindset, the right behaviour and knowledge of what you are doing, you can build wealth and end up rich.

Behaviour starts in the mind and can be entrenched through our habits. Some of us have learnt some rather bad ones along the way. Have you heard the expression, 'she can't work with money'? It's true – working with money, and making money work for you, is a skill. I was told many years ago that if you could live on R5 000 per month, then you would be able to live on R50 000 per month. I believe that – it's not how much money we have but what we do with it that is critical.

But why a book specifically for women? Money knows no gender, so why would a woman want to be treated any differently when it comes to her money? That's exactly the point. Women don't want to be treated differently at all, but the world of money still seems to be largely dominated by men.

Women earn less than men in South Africa – a staggering 30% less than their male counterparts doing the same job, according to Statistics South Africa's Inequality Trends report of 2019. No matter how far we have come in terms of equality, money talks and there is no excuse for this blatant discrimination. Many women are on the receiving end of gender-based violence, and money no doubt plays a role here: in many of these situations, a woman simply doesn't have the financial means to remove herself from a dire situation.

Around 54% of women are single parents, with only 20% receiving regular paternal support, according to the Old Mutual Savings and Investment Monitor of 2019. It's a tough road for many.

LIFE AT THE TOP

When we look at the world's richest people, it's clear that some have clawed their way to success, while others have been blessed with good inheritances. In the Forbes 35th Annual World Billionaires List published in 2021, out of the total of 2 755, only 328 were women – just under 12%. Jeff Bezos topped the list, followed by Elon Musk, Bernard Arnault and Bill Gates, with Mark Zuckerberg coming in at number five.

The world's richest woman, L'Oréal heiress Françoise Bettencourt Meyers, was followed by Walmart heiress Alice Walton and Jeff Bezos's ex-wife, MacKenzie Scott. Julia Koch, widow of David Koch, and Miriam Adelson, widow of casino boss Sheldon Adelson, followed. Each of these women inherited rather than built her fortune. By contrast, more than two-thirds of the men on the list built their wealth up from scratch.

The good news, though, is that the number of female billionaires is increasing. In 2017, only 8% (145) of the people on the list were women, which grew to 11.9% (328 women) in 2021. Closer to home, the richest woman in South Africa at the time of writing is Wendy Appelbaum (owner of De Morgenzon wine estate along with her husband Hylton). She is followed by Wendy Ackerman (Ackerman Family Trust), Irene Charnley (various directorships), Bridgette Radebe (mining, and sister of Patrice Motsepe), Sharon Wapnick (inherited), Elizabeth Bradley (directorships and daughter of the first person to bring the Toyota brand to South Africa) and Dr Judy Dlamini (chairperson of Mbekani Investment Holdings Limited and Aspen Pharmacare Holdings Limited), to name but a few.

Most of us will never make it onto a list of the richest, but it really is admirable when a woman does. It's been a man's world, but the balance of power continues to shift. Women today have many more opportunities compared to their mothers and grandmothers, but the reality of pay gaps, social challenges and women taking time off from their careers to have children means that the road to wealth can be much tougher for a woman than it is for a man.

Many South African women have broken through glass ceilings and prospered. But earning money is one thing; knowing how to make it work for you is an entirely different ballgame. Smartwoman knows this, and makes smart choices.

THE BATTLE OF THE SEXES

Is there a difference between how men and women view money, and does this affect a woman's ability to build wealth? A fair bit of research has been done in this space. For many years, the financial services industry has recognised that women remain a largely untapped market. A 2012 study conducted by Fidelity Investments (an American multinational financial services company) found that 70% of widows fire their financial advisers within one year of their spouse's death. The reason behind this was simple: the widows felt that their advisers were condescending towards them. Despite having had a long relationship with the family, the adviser often met with the husband only and, even in joint meetings, would communicate primarily with the husband. The widows felt little affinity with their advisers and believed they'd been overlooked and undervalued, leading to a lack of trust.

The focus of the research in itself was interesting to me: it assumed that the wealth in the family had been accumulated by the husbands. I couldn't help wondering why the research had not been done on the widows as investors in their own right. It does reflect reality, though, which is why I have included it here: the reality of how the financial services industry views women as needing advice only when widowed or divorced. Which, of course, is utter nonsense. Women build wealth throughout their careers and lives. They need professional advice all along the way, not only when there is no longer a man around!

But back to the question: Do men and women view money differently? Is money not just money, with us all treating it the same? Maybe, maybe not. There is a theory that women view money as a lake, whereas men view it as a river. As a lake, it is finite and needs to be preserved. There is a fear that it might run out. As a river, it flows and rejuvenates itself endlessly. It will always be there, so one can afford to take more risks with it.

This is quite a generalisation, but there may be some truth in it. Maybe it goes back to the days of the caveman, when men would go out into the dangerous world to hunt for food while women stayed near the cave, experts at gathering and preserving whichever edible foodstuffs they could find. If the men didn't return from the hunt, the women faced the real possibility of starvation, hence the drive to preserve what little they had. Who knows? We have come a long way since then, but we still have many hidden drivers and habits that affect how we interact with money. We will explore these in more detail later.

As women, we are often generous and have a strong sense of community. Our interest in gathering money is driven both by what it can do for us (personal experiences) and how it can serve the needs of those we love. I think we are generally more giving than men, irrespective of social standing. Many women play an active role in uplifting people; one of the great benefits of having wealth, for these women, is the ability to give money away and help others. It's the old tithing concept in a more modern and independent context.

For men, money often represents power, prestige and a sense of achievement. They view money as a game, a way of keeping score, of measuring how well they are doing. More is always better, because money provides security, freedom and a way for them to achieve their goals. There are even books in which men speak about mastering the game of money!

When it comes to investing and taking action that can lead to wealth, men may take more risks (because there will always be money), whereas women may take more time, do more research and be steered into more socially responsible investments. Men may come across as more confident in their decisions, whereas women have longer time horizons and clearer goals. So, when women take more time, it just means that they make more informed decisions. We may be more risk averse than men, but we are generally more open to getting advice and gathering the relevant information before making investment decisions. Those of us who lack confidence in the world of investing will most probably invest through company-owned plans (such as retirement funds) or in a bank account.

There is a lot we can learn from one another when it comes to investing, but, as women, the last thing we want to do is operate like men.

Money is life and life is money, so the saying goes. It is impossible to separate our money from the joy of living. As we travel down the road of life, we face many unexpected situations that affect us, sometimes harshly. An event such as a divorce or retrenchment may throw us right off course. The important thing is to never adopt a victim mentality. Taking ownership of our finances is taking ownership of our futures.

There is no 'one size fits all'. Every woman's journey is different. But we all have one thing in common – a desire to accumulate wealth and live our best lives.

I was once told that creating wealth and getting rich is simple. All you have to do is spend less than you earn and invest the rest. Can't argue with that! But behind that statement lies a mountain of complexities. The world of money can be daunting, so many of us shy away from it. We may even have acquired habits that make us poorer instead of richer and, without realising it, we may be shooting ourselves in the foot.

But the Smartwomen of this world are one level up. They embrace the world of money, and money works for them. Their journey to financial success is based on a solid understanding of three critical areas:

- themselves – what drives them, how they view money, and what they need to do to achieve their goals;
- their environment – which external influences can have a negative or positive impact and how they can stay true to their goal; and
- the tools – the nuts and bolts of investing and how wealth is created.

Getting to grips with these three areas is the key to the door of wealth. There is a Smartwoman inside each of us, and I believe that curiosity distinguishes successful people from the rest. Be inquisitive. Actively seek information and keep learning. Grow your self-confidence. Challenge perceptions and question the things you have been told are true. Set your own goals. Surround yourself with positive people. Give back. Talk less, listen more. Find your own path and take the first step on your road to riches.

Chapter 2

The magic of money

'People say that money is not the key to happiness, but I always figured if you have enough money, you can have a key made.'

– Joan Rivers

Can money buy happiness? This is an age-old question. Money on its own has no value. If we lived in a fairy-tale world where we could have everything we wanted for free, no amount of money (or lack thereof) would matter. But that is not reality, and the value of money lies in what it can do for us. It is a tool – a very valuable means to an end. In the very early days, people used a barter system in which they exchanged food and other provisions. As communities evolved, this barter system became more complex, and the early forms of money started evolving. Today we have a highly sophisticated world of international currencies, exchange rates, electronic 'money' and varying forms of credit. But the fundamental process hasn't changed – money is still a form of exchange.

Think of it this way: You give your skills and time to an employer or business in exchange for money. You use that money to buy a lifestyle. So you are, in effect, a business of your own – you generate money that you use to buy yourself a lifestyle. Of course, you also have to consider the impact of your not being able to generate money. How would you fund your lifestyle? You would hopefully have accumulated enough wealth not to need that income any longer, but more about that in Chapter 25.

Money can be easy to take for granted, but the COVID-19 pandemic, in which many people found their incomes and businesses devastated, put a new perspective on money and the value it holds in our lives. It is often said that only when we lose something do we realise its worth. The worth of money is as a means to the lifestyle you value, irrespective of your income or social standing.

Logically, the more money you have, the better your lifestyle – at least in material terms. (Let's ignore other aspects, such as health, for the time being.) Much of our time and energy is taken up in the pursuit of money. We strive to get ahead, to get rich. 'Rich' means 'successful', and we all want to be successful. 'Rich' can mean opulence, being able to spend without worrying about where the money comes from. A bottomless pot of money. What 'rich' really means to most people is financial freedom – never having to worry about money again.

Money is also associated with happiness; many people believe they would be happier if they had more money. Not having enough money to live comfortably can be a great source of stress and unhappiness, as can losing your job and income.

Rich people are happier, as pointed out in 'Can money buy you happiness?', a November 2014 article in the *Wall Street Journal*. Research generally proves that affluent people are happier overall than those who struggle to make ends meet. But if we dig a little deeper, we can gain some interesting insights. Professor Ryan T. Howell, associate professor of psychology at San Francisco State University, found that wealth alone doesn't guarantee a good life. Life experiences play a far greater role in creating happiness. According to Howell's research, giving money away instead of spending it on themselves makes people feel happier. When people do spend money on themselves, experiences such as travel make them feel far happier than purchasing durable goods. Yet we have a natural tendency to spend money on goods – they are durable by nature, whereas experiences are fleeting. When people look back on where they have spent their money, however, they realise that experiences provide better value in the long run.

So, buying 'stuff' doesn't make us any happier, but having money to buy experiences can go a long way towards doing this.

How much money do we need, then, and at what point do we have enough? When I'm addressing audiences, I like to ask for a show of hands as to who earns, or has, enough money. Amidst some laughter, only one or two people will raise their hands. Generally speaking, none of us ever has enough money. The reason for this is simple – we always seem to believe that, if we had more money, things would be better, we would be happier, we would be able to do so much more with our lives. We live in the belief that if only we get promoted, or get a new job, or win the lottery, we'll have enough money.

But what happens in reality? When we get that promotion, or new job, or even win the lottery, we spend more. We move into a more expensive house, we buy a better car, we spend more on entertainment or travel. The more we earn, the more we spend. Along with this comes more debt: increased car financing, a bigger home loan and higher credit limits. It's a cycle we perpetuate, so we never really feel that we have 'enough'. We get caught on the treadmill of earning and owing, meaning we never reach a point of satiety. More importantly, we are not building wealth.

Bear in mind, too, that feeling that you have 'enough', or that you are comfortable (or even rich), is all relative. Some people are more materialistic than others. Others value giving back to the community. Some have a great fear of poverty in old age, so they save as much as they can. We are all different but, in general, we have a desire to own more, to earn more, to be financially comfortable, and perhaps even rich.

Having money can bring a different set of problems to the table, however. Once you have money, you need to keep it. You need to know how to manage it, treat it responsibly and make it work for you. How many people have won the lottery and found themselves wealthy beyond their dreams overnight, only to become penniless a few years later because they didn't look after their money? It happens more easily than one might imagine.

There are many well-known examples in the United Kingdom and the United States, but two local stories are really tragic. At the tender age of 19, Jason Canterbury from the Cape Flats won R6.7 million in 2003. For a few years he lived the good life, buying cars and property, but once his winnings evaporated, he turned to drugs and crime to support his lifestyle. In 2010, he was sentenced to 28 years in jail for murder.

In another case, a former policeman from Pietermaritzburg, Dayalin Maslamoney, won R10.4 million. He quit his job and enjoyed his newfound wealth. He divorced his wife, split what was left of his winnings and lost his share in a failed business venture. He ended up living in his ex-wife's house and working at one of her video rental shops.

The need for financial skills is universal, whether you get rich overnight or build your wealth slowly. Sadly, we are not taught these skills at school. Instead, we take our cue from our parents and what we see and experience around us. No wonder so many people end up with chronic debt and feel they are working merely to survive, stuck on a treadmill of earning and spending.

Another issue, of course, is that we often take what we have for granted. Our lotto winners never anticipated the day their money would run out. And although we may bemoan our meagre salaries or feel that we need more money to be fulfilled, we seldom consider that our situation might change for the worse. Hindsight is always clearer than foresight.

A former colleague of mine had an amusing perspective on taking money for granted. When she was married she lived in Constantia, an upmarket Cape Town suburb, enjoying all the trappings that her wealthy husband could provide without a care in the world for how things were being paid for. Then they divorced. Suddenly, she appreciated everything and saw money in its true context. She joked that her lifestyle had changed dramatically but that she had managed to keep a postbox in Constantia – the only property she will ever own there!

Most of us will never win the lottery. We have to work for a monthly income. What we do with this income is the critical thing. It is often the difference between people who are wealthy (the Smartwomen) and those who battle along from payday to payday.

Once a month, when our salaries are paid into our bank accounts, we may feel rich for a few days (or a few hours!), but our money starts disappearing as our debit orders run and we buy groceries, pay bills and cover other expenses. Soon things look pretty slim, and we wait for the next payday. Some of us haven't got a clue where all our money went, and repeat the cycle over and over again. Each month, we hope that we can make it through to payday – that we won't have more month than money on our hands.

The payday-to-payday lifestyle is easy to fall into. Yes, there may be excuses for why things aren't different (I can't afford to save; life is so expensive; prices just keep going up), but until you shift your thinking and start behaving differently, you will remain in this trap, wishing you were wealthy and admiring those who are.

The huge risk here, of course, is that your income is not guaranteed – it could dry up at any point. What then? How would you fund your lifestyle if you did not have a nest egg to fall back on? Even if you are busy building wealth, you still need to protect it to ensure your lifestyle.

Living from payday to payday and taking our money for granted means that we are neither making it work for us, nor treating it with any respect. For me, this lies at the core of building wealth, or creating financial freedom, or however you would like to label it. Taking your money seriously, treating it with respect and making it work for you, will set you free financially and give you choices in your life.

The opposite of freedom is restriction – being forced to stay on that treadmill, working to earn money because it flows out as fast as it comes in. You consume your money like oxygen: once it's used, it's gone. By contrast, making wise decisions and empowering yourself will put you on the path to financial freedom, the road to wealth. It creates the opportunity to do things that you *want to do*, not that you *have to do* to survive.

We do not build wealth in a vacuum but in the context of our wonderful and unpredictable lives. We may face many different challenges along the way, and some situations may throw us off course, no matter how determined we are. When it comes to life, one size does not fit all. This is equally true when it comes to growing wealth. Knowledge is power, as they say, so it all starts with learning and understanding. That will lead you to the right actions, which will lead you to the right results.

Chapter 3

Smart thoughts lead to success

'Success isn't about how much money you make;
it's about the difference you make in people's lives.'
— *Michelle Obama*

Ask ten people what they think is the best way to get rich, and you will get ten different answers. Each person will think that they're right, and may defend their position vehemently, illustrating the fact that we have different views about money and that this shapes our actions.

Just as we think, feel and behave differently due to our individual personalities, we also have different *money* personalities. Our personal beliefs and values about money directly affect our interactions with it. This, in turn, positively or negatively affects our efforts to build wealth. Based on our beliefs, we develop habits that become wired into our brains, so much so that we think they are normal for everyone – or that they should be!

Consider your circle of acquaintances. You may have that one friend who turns every rand over three times before spending it, and another who throws caution to the wind and lives for today. Neither friend is right or wrong – they just have different money personalities and values. Understanding how we view money subconsciously gives us greater insight into ourselves, and may help us identify behaviours and thought patterns that are counterproductive. We may need to unlearn old habits and develop new ones on our road to building wealth.

But let's take a step back. Where and how are these thought patterns formed? Psychologists disagree about whether they are caused more by genetics or upbringing, but there is no doubt that children learn from what they see. We have learnt from our parents – and, equally so, transmit messages to our children – about money and how to deal with it.

I grew up in a single-parent household, where it was imprinted on my brain that a woman needs to take care of herself financially. The idea of relying on a man never really entered my frame of reference. Money was not to be taken for granted, and we didn't buy anything on credit. We didn't have lots of money – there was definitely no money tree in our garden – but grew up with the perception that it needed to be treated with respect and spent with caution.

I started working as a teenager, doing casual jobs during school holidays, then part-time work and holiday jobs while studying at the University of Cape Town. I always saved like crazy, and was able to buy my first car in cash at the age of 20. It took me four years to save that whopping R1 500 (equivalent to roughly R26 500 today). So, from a young age, I had a healthy relationship with money that I have maintained throughout my adult life: I valued it and viewed it with respect.

The world is a rather different place today. We seldom use cash and no longer carry chequebooks. Instead, we use cards to pay when shopping, or we shop online. Accounts are paid electronically via internet banking, often via a banking app on our phone. Money is not as tangible as it once was; it's largely just a series of numbers on a screen. This makes it easy to spend and overspend. Debt is rife. The 1980s ushered in the credit card – credit had been available at some clothing stores before that, but we used cash for the vast majority of our shopping. The advent of credit cards meant increased turnover for businesses, as a lack of cash was no longer a deterrent to consumers.

Most of us do not remember those pre-credit days, when people had to budget tightly and stick to it. Some may recall the 'envelope system', which entailed managing the household budget by putting money into separate envelopes, each intended for a specific purpose. There would be a grocery envelope, a travel envelope, a rent or bond envelope, and so on. When the envelope was empty, the money was finished, forcing families to budget carefully and spend with caution.

Today, money seems so much more freely available. Just look at any shopping mall over weekends: for many teenagers, shopping and hanging out at the mall is a regular pastime (or at least used to be, before the COVID-19 pandemic struck). This is a relatively new phenomenon – our parents were not given money to go and entertain themselves for hours at malls. Malls didn't exist as they do today, and certainly did not provide a 'shoppertainment' element. Entertainment had a very different format, and shopping was driven largely by necessity. Today, the very fact that we can spend an entire day at a shopping mall with our children creates a spending culture from a young age.

INSTILLING MONEY VALUES IN OUR KIDS

Children learn from their parents in all respects, and what they see and experience can leave a lasting impression on them. If parents are frugal, children may feel that others have more than them. As adults, they may break out of that headspace, spending and enjoying their money – the opposite of what they experienced as children. If parents spoil children by giving them everything they want, children may grow up feeling entitled, running the risk of spending far more than they earn. Awareness of these issues can go a long way towards teaching children a healthy attitude towards money.

Some people don't seem to have a clue how to work with money. They just spend, enjoying today and having little to show for it tomorrow. Others may not like talking about money in the household, so they pass no financial knowledge on to their children. These children become adults who have to learn to manage their money through trial and error. Parents can pass their biases and attitudes on to their children without realising it. If a parent badmouths banks, for example, their children grow up with a negative perception of banks, never trusting them. A cynical view of investing or the finance industry may leave children believing the same, rightly or wrongly.

The things parents say can carry a huge amount of weight in a child's eyes. As a teenager, I was told by a friend's father that he did not believe in saving money for his children – he had earned it, and it was there to be enjoyed. Tomorrow will take care of itself, was his motto. I lost contact with that friend, but I've wondered how this affected her and where she is in life today. I found her father's attitude odd, to put it mildly, but he was loud and proud about it!

Household dynamics also affect how we see money. If your mother is or was financially dependent on your father, you may take your cue from that, subconsciously looking for Prince Charming. You may have studied and found a great job, but your ultimate goal will be to find a partner who earns more than you and can give you a better lifestyle than the one you can give yourself. I am not going to get sucked into the whole 'a man is not a financial plan' argument, but this remains a mindset that many women have – despite all the glass ceilings we've broken through.

I knew a woman who brought this home quite vividly. She had a good education and held a senior position in her company, but love seemed to elude her. She had had a few really bad relationships with men who were well-off financially. One day, someone joked that she was looking to marry a pension fund, meaning that a man's financial standing was the most important consideration for her.

Divorce can also have a huge impact on children. A child from a divorced home may be determined to get married and live happily ever after in the way their parents could not. They may get married in community of property, wanting to share everything, buy a house and start a family, pursuing all the elements that should make for a happy marriage.

It's good to recognise the influences that have shaped our attitudes and behaviour towards money, but doing so doesn't give us an excuse not to improve them. I don't believe in blaming one's parents or being a victim. We may have learnt some of our habits from our parents, and others from what we have seen and experienced, but we need to take responsibility for our own financial behaviour and make changes where we need to. Taking responsibility and control is a major part of growing wealth and getting rich. Avoid responsibility and your situation will stay the same, year in and year out.

We are both child and parent. If you have children, remember your responsibility to pass good money skills on to them. Lead by example, first and foremost. If you are teaching your child to budget with their pocket money, do so by using your own budget. You don't need to share all your financial information with your child, but explaining that you are saving for a big purchase instead of buying on credit, for example, will demonstrate the skill of budgeting. As your children grow older, teach them about credit and how to use it responsibly. Again, your personal behaviour must mirror your words.

Giving pocket money to kids is great, but there should also be a clear understanding of what they are to use this money for. You may agree to pay for certain things, while your children use their pocket money for airtime or entertainment, perhaps. Set clear boundaries around this and stick to your guns. If your child overspends, or spends all their pocket money in one day, don't bail them out by giving them more money. It's the worst lesson you can teach them – that someone will always bail them out. It can sow the seeds for poor money habits in adulthood. Although it may be a harsh lesson, it's invaluable.

Encourage your children to save from an early age. South Africa has a notoriously low rate of savings, and this can only change one family at a time. Christmas and birthday gifts often take the form of cash, especially as children get older and people are not sure what to buy them. They can spend some of it, but encourage an attitude of saving, particularly if they have a savings goal in mind. Open a savings account for them. You could even deposit their pocket money into this account. Early exposure to the world of banking and saving will allow them to experience the wonder of compound interest and the benefits of long-term savings.

A holiday job is also a great way of teaching financial independence from a relatively young age. It's fun and exciting to start earning your own money, and doing so allows children to save up for something really big that they want.

The world of debt will be waiting for unsuspecting teenagers, either as students or when they start working. It's a good idea to start talking about credit and explaining how it works as your children grow older. It is easy to fall into the debt trap if you're ignorant, and clever marketing campaigns have lured many young people into debt. Make time to have family discussions about debt and share your experiences (good and bad) with making decisions about debt. Your kids will learn from this.

BANK OF MOM AND DAD

The world can be a tough place to navigate. When our children fly the coop, we hope that they will have the tools not only to cope but to thrive. It's not always easy to let go as a parent – having to stand back and watch them learn the harsh lessons of life can feel near impossible, as our instinct is to save and protect our children, no matter the circumstance.

The journey into adulthood isn't always plain sailing. In many instances, adult children end up returning to the family home in the wake of a crisis such as divorce, retrenchment or, most recently, the COVID-19 pandemic. Apart from these unusual circumstances, there are many other situations in which adult children simply can't survive financially and end up repeatedly knocking on Mom or Dad's door for a loan or other financial help.

While you might feel you are doing the right thing as a parent by giving them money, you may be doing more harm than good. As children grow, their physical and emotional dependence on their parents changes. As parents, our love must adapt to this. The child must explore ways of coping with the challenges of life, and if the parent's love does not adapt, the child remains vulnerable, needy and possibly even helpless – what we call 'learned helplessness', which occurs when a person continuously faces a negative, uncontrollable situation and they stop trying to change their circumstances. This can lead to anger and rage on the part of the child, cause great emotional distress and upset the family dynamic. It can also be a drain on your pocket and threaten your own financial security. Once you reach the empty-nest stage, your expenses should decrease and you should really start ramping up your savings towards retirement. An ongoing financial drain can be financially devastating in your later years.

So, you need to be a little selfish and not neglect your own needs. If your adult children are living at home, they must contribute, no matter how small their contribution. If they need financial support, set boundaries and a timeline so that you are not continually shelling out money.

Only help out if you can afford it, and when you lend them money, set up a repayment plan and enforce it.

Parenting is one of the most challenging roles to play, as we don't always realise the massive impact of our behaviour on our children. Financial skills are as important as the other life skills we impart. When we take our money seriously and make it work for us, we create our own financial stability and security. In the process, we give our children one of the greatest gifts we can: skills that will allow them to prosper, no matter which direction they take.

But back to you: your parents and upbringing played a major role in your attitude to money. What is this attitude and how does it influence your behaviour? Let's examine this in more detail.

Chapter 4

Your money personality

'We first make our habits, then our habits make us.'
— *John Dryden*

The psychology of money is a broad and complex subject. A number of personality profiling tests aim to identify individual attitudes, emotions and habits towards money, which ultimately dictate how we approach spending and saving.

Money is a hugely emotional issue, despite the fact that it is a cold, inanimate – or digital – object. It represents different things to different people, ranging from security to status to power. It is even a facilitator for some, enabling them to help and uplift others. We all have different uses for money.

Examining our money personality is part of a journey of self-awareness and allows us an objective view of ourselves. We may not agree with every single aspect of the profiling test result, but it does give us greater insight into our approach to money. By identifying our beliefs and habits, we can identify what helps and hinders us in building wealth, and what we could do to find a new path.

It is also useful for couples to understand their respective money personalities, as this can cause huge clashes in a relationship if not discussed and explored. Two people may have very different values about money and both may believe that they are right, having never explored alternative perspectives. If you clash over finances with someone close to you, why don't both of you do the Money Personality Quiz here to gain some insight?

It's not a magic wand that will solve all of your problems, but it is an objective starting point for a discussion that will hopefully lead to an improved situation. Start by looking for common ground in your beliefs and goals, then build on that. If you cannot resolve these differences yourselves, then consider getting outside help from a money coach.

It is important to note that no test will ever be 100% accurate; what it provides is a general guideline. In most cases, the results do not come as too much of a surprise. However, you may find that you deny certain things about yourself, so discuss the results with someone close to you whom you trust, and then decide for yourself.

I have examined a number of money personality tests – some more intricate than others, and some just for fun (which the tests state upfront!). I like the Money Personality Quiz Liz Koh has developed. Koh runs a financial-planning business in New Zealand and is the author of *Your Money Personality: Unlock the Secret to a Rich and Happy Life* (published by Awa Press in 2008). I have found it to be fairly accurate, and the results are really useful.

Try it out!

MONEY PERSONALITY QUIZ

To work out your money personality, choose one answer for each question that is the best fit for you.

1. Most of my money is …
   a) owed to the bank due to maxed-out credit cards
   b) in the bank
   c) tied up in shares or property investments
   d) dedicated to my mortgage, new car or home renovations

2. If I won a million rand, I would …
   a) throw a party on a cruise ship for everyone I know
   b) put it in the bank and phone my adviser
   c) use it to set up that business on the side that I have been dreaming of
   d) buy a better house and car

3. **My philosophy on money is …**
   a) it doesn't come easy, so be careful with it
   b) you can't take it with you when you die, so you might as well live to the max
   c) you need it to surround yourself with things you love
   d) it comes and goes, and that's just the way it is

4. **My favourite way to spend spare time is …**
   a) shopping till I drop
   b) something that is fun, but free
   c) working on my house
   d) dreaming up a new business venture

5. **What I am most concerned about …**
   a) I earn plenty, but I don't have any savings to show for it
   b) I have all my money tied up in savings, but it's not really growing
   c) I don't mind taking risks with my money, but it does upset my loved ones
   d) I probably shouldn't shop so much, but I can't help myself

6. **Other people consider me to be …**
   a) a big spender
   b) careful with my money
   c) well-off because of my lifestyle
   d) a successful investor

7. **When I spend money, I buy …**
   a) mostly on impulse
   b) only after I have shopped around for the best price
   c) only what I need, because I would rather invest my money
   d) quality things that will last, even if they will cost a bit more

8. **My view of retirement savings is …**
   a) I save each payday for my retirement
   b) I'll get around to it when I've paid off my home loan or other debts
   c) I'm investing mostly in property and businesses for my retirement
   d) I don't need to save because someone else (or the government) will take care of me

9. When it comes to managing money …
   a) I'm hopelessly out of control
   b) I keep track of what I have got and how much I have spent
   c) I have a good income, but I don't know where all my money goes
   d) I take big risks, but they usually pay off

10. A friend wants you to invest R20 000 in an exciting new venture. You say …
    a) yes, even if you have to borrow the money
    b) yes, but only if you can afford it
    c) no, because it's too risky
    d) no, because if you had R20 000, you would rather spend it

11. When it comes to buying a house to live in …
    a) I can't save enough to buy the one I would like
    b) I would buy what I could easily afford
    c) I would buy the house I like, even if it's a struggle to pay the mortgage
    d) I would buy an average house to live in so that I can buy one or more investment properties as well

12. When it comes to credit cards …
    a) I either don't have one, or I have one and pay it off in full each month
    b) all my cards are maxed out
    c) I still have credit available and I pay off as much as I can each month
    d) I would borrow money on one for a good investment opportunity

Now score yourself:

Put a circle around the letters that correspond with your answer; for example, if you chose answer b) to question 1, then circle the letter H.

	a)	b)	c)	d)
1	T	H	E	A
2	T	H	E	A
3	H	T	A	E
4	T	H	A	E
5	A	H	E	T
6	T	H	A	E
7	T	H	E	A
8	H	A	E	T
9	T	H	A	E
10	E	A	H	T
11	T	H	A	E
12	H	T	A	E

Now add up how many times you circled each letter, and enter your scores in the boxes below:

H = HOARDER	
A = ACHIEVER	
E = ENTREPRENEUR	
T = THRILL SEEKER	

Interpreting your score

Everybody has elements from each money personality. The two in which you scored the highest will be the ones that mostly define your money personality. The one in which you score the highest is your dominant money personality.

Hoarders are very conservative money managers. They live by a strict budget and keep spending under tight control. Hoarders dislike debt and prefer to save up to buy things they want. They are content with their lot and will cut their coat according to their cloth. As a Hoarder, you will end up with a nice pile of cash in the bank, but if you are overcautious, you may miss out on using it to enjoy life more.

Achievers are status conscious and will spend money on things that create an impression of affluence and success, such as a home in one of the better suburbs, an expensive car, stylish furniture and overseas holidays. The challenge for an Achiever is being able to have an affluent lifestyle without accumulating too much debt.

Entrepreneurs are the true creators of wealth. They are prepared to take on an initially high level of risk in the expectation of high returns from investments in business or property. And if they don't have enough money of their own, they will use someone else's! As an Entrepreneur, your road to fortune will be smoother if you set aside part of your wealth in safe investments, rather than risking it all.

Thrill Seekers see money as a source of short-term satisfaction rather than something to be accumulated, and live by the motto 'easy come, easy go'. Spending gives them a buzz and their credit cards are usually maxed to the limit. Once the thrill of spending has worn off, Thrill Seekers often feel remorseful about their actions and overwhelmed by debt. As a Thrill Seeker, you will need to put strict controls on your budget and the amount of credit you have.[1]

Remember, there are only two things you can do with money – spend it or save it. Which traits did you identify, using the Money Personality Quiz, that may be hindering you when it comes to managing money? And which positive traits do you have that enable you to manage money better? Use the worksheet that follows to think about the changes you could make to get closer to achieving your dreams and goals.

---

[1] Reproduced with permission from *Your Money Personality: Unlock the Secret to a Rich and Happy Life*, Liz Koh, Awa Press, 2008. www.moneymax.co.nz/www.moneymaxcoach.com

WORKSHEET: MY MONEY PERSONALITY

My dominant money personality/ies	Positive traits	Negative traits	What can I change?

Chapter 5

Whose life is it anyway?

> 'There is a gigantic difference between earning a great deal of money and being rich.'
>
> *– Marlene Dietrich*

What we do with our money – how much of it we spend and how much of it we save – is influenced on different levels. Subconsciously, our money beliefs, values and habits drive certain behaviours. But many external influences also compete for their share of our wallet. Being smart means becoming aware of this; it is the first step in making positive changes that will put you on the road to wealth.

The first and probably most impactful influence is that we live in a consumer society that encourages us to spend at every opportunity. Successful people are able to spend money to acquire things, and we all want to be seen as successful.

So, what is success? We are constantly bombarded with messages that define it: stick-thin models splashed across magazines; images of homes and furnishings that are to die for; fabulous clothes; beautiful cars and holidays that we all deserve. These things show the world that we have 'arrived'.

It's not always about owning these symbols of success: the mere act of shopping for them can give us great pleasure, too. We all like to do things that make us feel good and get us recognised. The hunting and comparing, the bargaining and the ultimate satisfaction – even euphoria – of making a purchase leaves us with a great sense of achievement. Our actions may defy logic, but that's because they are driven by our emotions; we do what 'feels' right, even if it isn't, from an affordability perspective.

Although we can control our reactions, we can't control what emotions arise within us, and we may fall easily into the trap of 'I own, therefore I am', building our self-worth on what we possess instead of who we are. That is not smart. We would never walk around bragging about how much money we have stashed away, but material possessions are highly visible, so they speak for themselves, giving us a certain aura of status. It's a way of making our success – or the illusion of it – easy for others to see.

The fact that we derive pleasure from hunting for and buying desirable items is not a sign of weakness. You may be surprised to learn that there is quite a bit of science behind it, in the area called neuroscience – the study of how the brain and nervous system interact, and how this affects our behaviour. Marketers and retailers have used the findings in a relatively new field called neuromarketing. It's a study of human behaviour that tracks the brain's responses to various marketing stimuli (packaging, advertising or other marketing activities) in the process of encouraging consumers to purchase. While the field of marketing may have tapped into these primal instincts in the past, our understanding of human behaviour is now far more intimate and calculated, because it's based on scientific research, as opposed to the marketer's instinct.

The first marketing and communication agencies specialising in this area sprung up at about the turn of the century. Today, neuromarketing is a buzzword in the marketing industry.

In his book *The Brain Sell: When Science Meets Shopping*, Dr David Lewis outlines some of the ways in which neuromarketing is used to get us to spend more. We know there are things we need and things we want, but if we want something strongly enough, we start to believe that we actually *need* it. I love perfume and always joke that I don't feel fully dressed unless I'm wearing it. Logically, I do not need perfume. Gone are the days when women had to disguise the odours that were the result of bathing only once a week! Yet my emotional connection with wearing perfume has blurred the line between need and desire – I 'need' to wear it to feel ready to face the day, so I perceive perfume as a need and not a want.

Blurring the lines between wants and needs leads to an emotion so powerful that consumers have to satisfy it, no matter the cost. Creating these need-wants in consumers, according to Lewis, is what retailers fantasise about. He goes on to say that some of the tactics for doing this include making the shopper work for the product (they must hunt to find the bargain); implying a sense of scarcity (that there is a limited number of these items available); suggesting an inadequacy (you have a flaw, but using this product will eliminate it); and making the buying process fun (shopping malls that offer a 'shoppertainment' experience are a classic example of this – you buy more because you spend more time in the mall due to the entertainment factor).

We also all know that the 'feel' of shops varies greatly. Supermarkets have wide aisles and are brightly lit, whereas an exclusive boutique may have subtle lighting and beautiful chairs for you to relax in and rest your weary legs! There is an art to all of this, and its goal is to design an experience aimed at getting you, the consumer, to spend more.

In 1973, Philip Kotler, professor of marketing at Northwestern University, Illinois, coined the term 'atmospherics' to describe the physical experience you have when you walk into a shop – the layout, temperature, lighting, noise level and décor. According to Lewis, some of the less obvious physical elements include lighting and colour. Blues and greens are calming, whereas red and dark colours increase stress and tension. Music plays a very important role in creating atmosphere, even if shoppers don't remember what was playing. Fast-paced music makes shoppers move around the space quickly, whereas slower music encourages them to linger and browse.

When it comes to grocery shopping, supermarket layouts are cleverly designed to entice you to spend more. According to Paco Underhill, consumer expert and author of the book *Why We Buy: The Science of Shopping*, as much as 70% of what we purchase in-store is unplanned. Supermarket layouts are intended to trigger impulse buying. Trolleys are placed at the entrance, while hand baskets are placed a little deeper inside the store. With a trolley you have more space to fill, so you are likely to spend more.

Most of us have lost the battle as soon as we step into the supermarket. Once inside, the first things you spot are the flowers and fresh produce. It looks good, feels good and evokes happiness. Happy customers spend more. Delicious smells from the bakery will make you hungry, and a hungry shopper buys more. You will have to battle your way through colourful displays and tempting products to get to the essential products such as milk, eggs and meat, which are always placed at the very back of the store.

Another crucial aspect is brand loyalty. How often do you insist on buying a particular brand, even if there is a cheaper one on the same shelf? It may be something as mundane as a cleaning agent or toilet paper. Brand loyalty is incredibly valuable for any retailer. I remember my university marketing lecturer speaking about toothpaste in the context of consumer goods and branding. All toothpastes meet the same need – to clean our teeth. All are pretty minty. Some promise whiter teeth as a bonus. Others are better if you want to kiss someone. Yet we all have our favourites and are loyal to a particular brand, whether this loyalty is due to the actual product (which are all fairly similar) or some other aspect.

Emotional engineering is what it's all about, because a consumer's personal connection to a brand is what creates customer loyalty. The use of images, slogans, music, words and other elements elicit an emotional response. When we consume a product, we get emotionally involved too, either positively or negatively. Pleasurable experiences, good feelings and our imagination all play a vital role in determining our emotions about a product. If the experience is positive, we want to repeat it. We become loyal to a brand because we want to feel pleasure over and over again. It's that simple. Emotional engineering creates a powerful bond between the consumer and the brand, and we may spend more money on an item simply because we are brand loyal.

So, the fact that we enjoy shopping is not a sign of weakness. Instead, it's a massive success story of clever marketing and manipulation by retailers and marketers. We are encouraged to spend and are rewarded by pleasurable experiences. What more could we want?

How many people do you know who spend the whole day at a shopping mall? And how often have you gone into a shop intending to purchase one item, then ended up with three or more? It's all in the science of retailing and the pleasure we derive from shopping – retail therapy!

The COVID-19 pandemic has had a major impact on shopping patterns, with a distinct move towards online shopping. In 2020, online shopping in South Africa rocketed by 66%, as many people exchanged malls for home deliveries. In 2018, R14 billion worth of retail goods were sold online (1.4% of all retail sales), and in 2020 this more than doubled to R30 billion. In 2021, online sales are expected to top R40 billion and account for 4% of all retail sales. We're buying everything online, from clothing and groceries to gifts, jewellery, pet accessories and books.

The more we shop online, the more we are bombarded with special offers, must-have getaways and the latest products. Online, we have access to far more information and reviews – or complaints – from other customers. Our purchases are more informed, but on the downside, being able to click and shop has made it much easier to spend. Our digital footprints are monitored and traced at a micro level, and targeted advertisements and special offers are served up every time we go online. We often make purchasing decisions with a single click.

The upside to technology is that it allows us to closely track our money and spending through online banking and budgeting apps such as 22seven. Managing our money and tracking our spending has never been easier, yet so many people still seem perplexed about where their money went.

THE BALANCING ACT

A major implication of our consumer and spending culture is the need to balance our needs today with our needs tomorrow. We have finite resources – a single fixed income, for most of us – and we need to make them cover all our bases.

With all the focus on today it is very easy to forget about tomorrow. Yes, there are many advertisements punting various investments, property deals, unit trusts or other forms of investing, but these are often placed alongside far more exciting messaging that offers instant pleasure. It's just not thrilling to think about the more distant future, unless you are planning something exciting, like a holiday.

It's not that we don't realise the need to save; people frequently ask me how much they should be saving. However, the answer is not clear-cut. The figure of 10% of your income is often bandied about, but it's not that simple. To build wealth, we need to set goals and have a plan in place, so several factors influence the answer to the question of how much to save. If you are talking about how much you should have for an emergency fund, a minimum of three months' take-home pay is usually recommended.

The real issue, though, is that many people struggle to find the money to save or invest. Their argument is that life is expensive and there is just no money to spare. Yet there is a savings culture among the lowest earners in South Africa – the stokvel. Stokvel members manage to find money to save, despite the fact that they may earn far less than people who claim they can't save. So, it's less about what you earn and more about your priorities. If your priorities are skewed entirely towards today's needs and wants, you will not have money to save and you will neglect your needs of tomorrow.

But life is tougher today than it was for previous generations, you may be thinking. Remember your parents' or grandparents' generation, in which only one person in the household worked? Yet they managed to raise children, educate them, live a fairly comfortable life and perhaps even go on an annual holiday. All on one income. In contrast, many dual-income households today find it difficult to make ends meet. Life seems so much more expensive. Could this be because we have more 'stuff', because our lifestyles are more complex, and because many things we once regarded as luxuries are now 'must-haves'? Our homes have two or more bathrooms, we often have two cars, we have credit cards, we eat out regularly, we spend, we consume. Compared to life 40 or 50 years ago, we own a lot more and also spend a lot more. Whether we are any happier, however, is a different discussion altogether.

We must also note that not all households have dual incomes. Some people live alone and do quite well on their single income. Others are single parents – it is estimated that more than half of all parents in South Africa are raising children on their own. This is a staggering figure, and presents huge financial challenges. Yet even a single parent needs to survive today and build wealth for tomorrow – just on a smaller scale, perhaps, than the dual-income household.

YOUR SELF-WORTH

Basing our self-worth on what we own and how we look, rather than on who we are, is an easy trap to fall into. The entire beauty industry is built on feeding our insecurities as women. We are told that we need to spend money on products such as fake nails and eyelashes, hair extensions, diet supplements, anti-aging skincare and whatever else can be dreamt up, as we need to conform to images of perfection that bombard us daily. We are never good enough and therefore need to shell out hard-earned cash to conform. I do believe that, as women, we empower ourselves through the way we dress and present ourselves, but there is a fine line between owning your style and being such a slave to fashion and expectation that it becomes a financial priority. This is not healthy or balanced.

When it comes to our careers, many of us are so busy running the rat race, competing at work and climbing that success ladder that we risk losing touch with who and what we really are, believing that our lives are 'normal'. We are not our possessions, we are not our job title, and we are definitely not the Joneses or Motsepes next door. Smartwomen know this.

If you link your self-worth to your job title, it can be a real problem when that job falls away. It's one of the challenges people face when they retire or are retrenched. Suddenly, they lose their sense of identity – without a job title they feel that they are no longer contributing to society. One of the first questions we often ask when we meet someone new is, 'What do you do for a living?' Our answer gives us meaning and validation, and can roll off our tongues without a second thought.

This was a challenge I faced when I left the corporate world. I'd spent many years as a marketing manager, and people understood this profession easily. Once I left that safe space and people asked me what I did, it took real effort not to say 'marketing manager' almost automatically. It took some sincere time alone and deep thought to come up with a meaningful reply.

It doesn't really matter what your title is, though. What is critical is that you have an inner sense of yourself and your significance, and of the contribution you make to your family, your community and society at large. I have little time for egos, and love the way the singer Frank Ocean puts it: 'Work hard in silence and let success be your noise.'

LOOK AT ME, I'VE ARRIVED!

The more we earn, the more we spend. Sadly, it's human nature. When we get the promotion or the new job with a killer salary, we move to a better suburb, buy a better car or shop at exclusive boutiques. When I was promoted to a management position many years ago, a senior colleague (a manager himself) joked that now I could no longer buy my groceries at Checkers, which was known for its low prices in those days. 'Heaven forbid,' he said. 'Imagine if someone saw you walking out of Checkers on a Sunday morning, pushing a trolley full of groceries!' As a manager, he reckoned, I should rather shop at Woolworths – far more upmarket and befitting of my new status. He may have said this in jest, but there is a huge amount of truth behind it: the snobbery of 'arriving', and the need to live up to it.

One cannot ignore the immense power of social media when it comes to showing the world what we have. We're no longer satisfied with showing our immediate circle of friends what we have acquired, where we go and how much fun our lives are; we can now put it out there for the world to see. Again, this earns us some kind of 'recognition', which we measure in likes, views and comments – who is seeing what we post, and how are they reacting?

SMALL CHANGES, BIG IMPACT

We often ignore the cost of these symbols of success, but they have a direct impact on our ability to grow our wealth. Let's look at one classic status symbol – the motor car. There are many different brands, and marketers have invested years and massive sums of money into creating unique features to ensure brand loyalty. The price of this brand perception is often far higher than the vehicle's actual value. When you buy a particular brand, you are not only buying the ability to commute from one place to another. You are also buying safety, convenience and, of course, the specific image that accompanies the brand.

Cars seem to say so much about a person, or so we believe. It's always been interesting to me that, when we start dating someone new, our friends generally ask three questions: What do they do for a living? Where do they live? And: What car do they drive? The car is right up there in importance, symbolising the person's status in society. In addition to the status element, there is the urban legend that you should trade your car in every two to three years so that it doesn't lose value. All this means is that you will remain beholden to a car finance company for your entire life! I've heard people say outright that they want to drive a new car every second year. It's part of how they measure their success. But, considered logically, this approach is short-sighted and unwise. Cars are made to last for many years, and the only return you get on the money you spend on a car is the 'status' of being seen to drive it.

From a financial perspective, that new car starts losing value the moment you drive it out of the showroom. Most cars depreciate at the rate of 15 to 20% per year, although this rate decreases as the car gets older. After five years, a car is generally worth half of what you paid for it. If you paid interest on it, that new car costs you dearly in two ways.

A 2013 article titled 'How car depreciation affects the value of your car' projects the depreciation of a new BMW, which is generally considered a luxury brand that depreciates considerably less than many other brands. This particular model BMW was worth R363 052 at the time of publication, and the depreciation was projected over the next five years. The numbers may be a few years old, but they still illustrate the issue perfectly:

Example: Vehicle deprecation in numbers

BMW 3 Series: (R363 052)	Year 1	Year 2	Year 3	Year 4	Year 5
Value	R308 594	R268 476	R241 629	R219 882	R202 292
Depreciation (%)	15%	13%	10%	9%	8%
Total loss	R54 458	R40 118	R26 847	R17 590	R16 184

A quick check of the cost in 2017 of a 2013 BMW 3 Series proves that these depreciation projections were fairly accurate. Over five years, the total loss in value due to depreciation is a staggering R155 197. In 2021, the same car is worth around R155 000 – a loss of around 58% of its value over eight years.

A car is not an investment – it's a money drain. Smartwomen know this. The more expensive the car, the more it costs you in monthly repayments and interest, and the more counterproductive it is to building wealth. Insurance premiums are also higher for expensive cars. There is simply no financial gain to be made by buying a more expensive car. Quite the opposite, in fact: doing so makes you poorer!

When it comes to buying a car, there is an array of financial options. Let's take a simplified look at the effect of buying cheaper or more expensive cars. I am assuming a 10% deposit and 9% interest rate, with the loan repayable over 60 months. Fees charged by the finance providers (such as admin or initiation fees) are excluded.

Example: Vehicle-financing implications

Car price	Deposit paid	Finance amount	Monthly repayment	Total interest paid	Total cost of car*
R100 000	R10 000	R90 000	R1 868	R22 095	R112 095
R150 000	R15 000	R135 000	R2 802	R33 143	R183 143
R200 000	R20 000	R180 000	R3 737	R44 190	R224 190
R250 000	R25 000	R225 000	R4 671	R55 238	R305 238
R300 000	R30 000	R270 000	R5 605	R66 285	R366 285

* Includes the interest paid

For every R50 000 you borrow, you pay roughly R934 more in monthly repayments. So, if you compare two cars costing R150 000 and R250 000:

- Repayments are R1 869 more per month for the pricier car.
- Assuming you paid the car off in five years, the total cost (including interest paid) of the pricier car is R122 095 more than that of the cheaper car.
- Insurance has not been factored in, but this cost will increase according to the price of the car.
- If you compare the prices of any two cars, it becomes clear that the more expensive the car you buy, the poorer you will make yourself over the long term.

Let's take car finance one step further. If you are in the market to buy a car, you have two choices – you can buy the more expensive car, or you can buy a cheaper car (new or a good second-hand car) and invest the difference of R1 869 per month. Let's ignore the additional insurance costs for this example. What would that money be worth over time? That is the real issue here – the opportunity cost of using that R1 869 for something else, such as an investment.

If you invested this money at an average growth rate of 12% per annum compounded monthly, and without ever increasing the contribution, look what you could accumulate:

Net value and buying power of an investment over time

Number of years invested	Net value	Buying power in today's terms, adjusted for inflation of 5.2%
5 years	R151 583	R117 644
10 years	R418 723	R252 214
15 years	R889 515	R415 831
20 years	R1 719 213	R623 756

By making a simple choice early in life, you could build up the equivalent of well over half a million rand, in today's value, over 20 years. This is money for nothing, generated from money that would otherwise have disappeared into your monthly budget. By making clever choices you could increase your wealth tremendously over time.

These numbers are based on an average growth of 12% per annum. Obviously, the better the growth you achieve, the greater the end result.

Play around with the numbers before you commit to buying a car, whether new or second-hand. There are some great calculators on websites such as www.automark.co.za or www.cars.co.za, or their easy-to-use apps. Just because you can afford to repay a certain amount every month doesn't mean you should buy for the maximum amount.

One last word of caution when purchasing a car: avoid balloon payments. While this payment structure makes your monthly instalment seem more affordable, it's never a smart idea in the long run. Buying a car with a balloon payment means that you pay the deposit at the end, instead of upfront, so your loan amount is less, resulting in reduced instalments. This makes it attractive. There are two nasty catches, though. Firstly, the interest you pay is calculated on the full amount (loan plus balloon portion). Generally, the interest would reduce over time as the loan balance decreases, but because the balloon portion doesn't decrease (you are only paying off the capital on the loan), you end up paying much more interest than if you had taken a standard car finance plan. Secondly, you will still need to repay the balloon amount at the end of the contract period, so you either have to sell the car (and hope the resale value will be sufficient to cover the cost of the balloon payment) or refinance the car. The only winners in this scenario are the car finance companies – for the consumer, it's simply a huge waste of money.

So, making the right choices in life has a profound effect on our ability to grow wealth. We all know that we can choose to drive a cheaper car or live in a more affordable area, but human nature tends to default to the belief that if we can afford it, we must have it – often at a huge long-term cost.

DESIGNER STUFF OR DESIGNER LIFE?

Despite all the pressure to which I have been exposed, along with so many others, I have always been a great believer in creating my own designer life as opposed to acquiring designer stuff. It's a mindset change and, when people catch on to it, it's incredibly empowering, because the simple truth is that accumulating stuff won't bring you happiness. The act of shopping may be pleasurable, but striving to acquire more and more things as badges of success ultimately has little meaning. Your focus should be on finding happiness in life, not happiness through buying things.

Comparing ourselves to everyone else (according to what society tells us is normal) can lead to massive feelings of inadequacy, of somehow missing out. FOMO – fear of missing out – can become very real when you strive to compete with others, and you may end up feeling inadequate when you can't keep up.

Living your designer life means that you live the life that you value. You spend your money in areas that are important to you, without trying to be like everyone else, influenced by what society tells you is important. It's about not comparing yourself to others. It's about setting your own rules, feeding your own passion and creating your own happy space. If growing your wealth is important, live accordingly.

Two vivid examples of people living their designer lives spring to mind. The first person I encountered many years ago, when I was fresh out of university. I'd just started a job and was eager to earn good money, get myself established and set up my first home. The manager in the department adjacent to ours was a man about 15 years my senior. One day, a colleague told me over coffee that he lived in a lower-income area, not far from the office. It was not a great suburb, and its many semi-detached houses had been built decades ago. We both thought it was really weird: he was a manager, for heaven's sake, and probably earned five times what we did!

A while later, my colleague told me that this man owned a yacht and that sailing was his passion. Suddenly it all made sense to me. His priorities were clear. He had a simple home so he could afford a yacht, and then lock up and go whenever he wanted to be out sailing. He was not conforming to society's expectations; he was living *his* designer life. A few years later, he resigned and sailed off to start a charter business in the Caribbean.

My second encounter with a designer life was a few years ago, when a friend told me excitedly that she had met her new boyfriend's parents over Sunday lunch. They lived in a middle-class suburb and had very humble furnishings and quite an old car, but went overseas on holiday once a year. Again, they clearly spent their money on what they valued – travel – and not on what society told them to value.

I am sure that in your own circle of friends and acquaintances there is a range of personalities, from those who save to those who are helping their parents financially, to those who blow all their money on socialising, buying the latest fashion items and other material possessions. There is no right or wrong way, but what is important is that it is *your* life that you are living, not someone else's. It may not be easy, given all the influences to which we are subjected, but a key element to building long-term wealth and getting rich is to spend your money on the right things. Build *your* designer life and stop squandering money on what you think your life *should* look like.

Sadly, some people only alter their behaviour after experiencing the negative consequences of their financial decisions. Be proactive and be smart. Don't wait to be hit by debt or tragedy. Live your life and spend your money wisely; small changes can make a big difference.

Chapter 6

Creating your designer life

'Being rich is having money. Being wealthy is having time.'
— *Margaret Bonnano*

As women, it's easy for us to get caught up in the craziness of life. The multiple roles we need to juggle – mother, partner, boss, employee, sister, daughter, and so on – can leave us reeling, with little time to focus on what is important to us and where we are headed. Sometimes, it's helpful to take a step back and assess what is really important – what we value and what we want out of life. Instead of following others blindly and being driven by consumerism, we can make smart choices to start growing our wealth – and getting rich!

For some, the act of shopping can relieve stress. Shopping is a bit of 'me-time', which is the basis of the retail-therapy argument. Buying things is also a form of reward – I've heard many women say, 'I work hard, so I deserve this.' This is all good and well if you really need the item and are buying it with cash, but if you're buying stuff you don't need with money you don't have, there is something wrong with the picture. In the long term it solves nothing, as you have not addressed the real cause of your stress or unhappiness. Also, many people reach a point in their lives when they want to start decluttering, getting rid of all the stuff they've accumulated to live a more minimalistic life. So much money has been poured into buying items that we simply send off to the charity shop. Another issue we cannot ignore is the need to be acknowledged and recognised, to be seen as unique and different. Very few of us want to blend into the background; self-help mantras tell us that we are special and unique, and on social media we can be the stars of our own show. Social media channels provide a soapbox on which to stand and proclaim ourselves to the rest of the world (or to our friends online, anyway). We can be whoever we want the world to think we are. The term 'Fakebook' has been coined to indicate that people can portray almost any image online.

Social media aside, we define ourselves in many other ways. It all depends on what we value as individuals. I have often heard someone being labelled a 'loser' if they don't conform to what society deems successful, usually in terms of their job and material possessions. Often, we fail to look more deeply at the person, who may, in fact, be living their designer life with little care for what society considers 'normal'.

Then there is the concept of a 'personal brand', a term that refers to the way that, in this cluttered, crowded world, we each portray an image, which defines how others perceive us. The term 'branding' is used frequently in the business world, but it applies to people too. It's about what we stand for and how we are perceived by others, and can be a direct reflection of our designer life.

Money is at the core of all this, because living up to society's expectations, and surrounding ourselves with the trappings of success, costs money. Yet, by being smart, we can satisfy our own needs, create our own designer life and make sure we end up rich.

FOUR PILLARS OF LIFE

Before we attempt to carve out our designer life it is important to realise that we cannot view our money or wealth in isolation. It is only one of the four pillars of our lives, the other three being physical health, mental health and relationships. Our well-being as individuals depends on keeping these pillars in balance. We neglect any one of them at our peril.

Like the legs of a table, the four pillars provide stability and resilience, allowing us to cope with whatever life throws at us. When they are balanced, they also allow us to find a sense of purpose, to be successful and, ultimately, to be happy. Focusing too much energy on one pillar can lead to problems in other areas of our lives.

If you focus primarily on wealth, you might become a workaholic, neglect your health, and begin to view relationships merely as tools for accumulating more power and money. It distorts your sense of purpose. You may end up rich, but feel unhappy and unfulfilled in other aspects of your life.

Illness can force you to focus exclusively on your health while neglecting the other pillars. This can be financially devastating and severely challenging to your mental health, as the battle against illness is as much physical as it is mental. We may neglect our relationships with friends, family and partners in the process. Similarly, being obsessed with your health can result in a beautiful body but leave you financially vulnerable, as you spend vast amounts of money in pursuit of the perfect body and develop an identity based entirely on how you look, instead of how you interact with others. This can damage your relationships.

Some people may have an intense focus on their mental growth, spirituality and understanding of themselves and the world around them, believing that mastering this will meet all the needs in other areas of their lives. This seldom happens; the results of this intense focus are weak relationships, no financial foundation and, perhaps, poor physical health. The only people who seem to be able to live a healthy life focused primarily on spirituality and mental growth are people in a religious order, such as monks and nuns.

If all your energy goes into your relationships and you constantly hunt for the perfect partner or obsess about family or friends, you are likely driven by your emotions and may easily neglect other aspects of your life. You may find yourself spending lots of money to impress and gain acceptance, leaving you financially weak. Your health may suffer and your poor perception of yourself may drive you to seek external validation, undermining the relationships you focus on so intensely.

That said, no one is perfectly balanced. We are a constant work in progress and our focus may shift from one pillar to another, depending on our circumstances. For example, if you are retrenched, the bulk of your energy will shift to the wealth pillar, as you need to find employment. But even though we tend to focus on one or two pillars at a time, based on our circumstances, it is important not to neglect any one of them in the longer term. It's all about balance. Being reasonably healthy in all four areas can go a long way towards creating our designer lives. It's not just about building our wealth or getting rich, but about doing so in the context of a balanced and healthy life.

How do you achieve that balance and define your own designer life? Here are some pointers. Remember, the power really is in your hands.

STEPS TO CREATE YOUR DESIGNER LIFE

1. Know what you want

If you don't know where you are going, how will you know when you get there? Have a clear picture in your mind about where you want to be and what you want to achieve, as this has a huge effect on your state of mind. Whether your goals are professional, personal or spiritual, we all need direction and guidance.

Coupled to the previous question are these: What gives you pleasure? Where do you find joy and happiness in life? The answers differ from person to person. I find immense joy in writing and gardening. We all have our happy spaces. Identify yours, then feed and nurture them.

When it comes to goals, waiting to see where life takes you could leave you frustrated, depressed and angry. With nothing against which to measure your progress, you may find yourself following someone else's agenda, abiding by somebody else's decisions and being easily swayed. You could end up spending valuable money on things that add little value to your life. What makes you happy and what you want to achieve may have no financial implications at all, but don't waste money on substitutes. Know what you value and want – whether it is financial or not – and draw up a plan to get there. (We examine dreams and goals in more detail in Chapter 12.)

2. Value who you are and what you do

How you view yourself and your role in the world is key to your mental health. It's the old self-confidence issue and, for me, it is one of the saddest things to see a woman devalue herself. This usually happens in the words she uses to describe herself, or what she doesn't say about herself. If we don't value ourselves, how will other people value us?

I'm sure we have all encountered women who sell themselves short, but one situation will stay with me forever. I worked with a middle-aged woman who was a little overweight, but attractive and intelligent, with a really pleasant personality. One day we were talking about relationships, and I asked her if she was married or involved with someone. Off the cuff, she replied, 'No. Look at me. Who would want me?' Her answer hit me between the eyes. She had made up her mind, so she would stay single. I saw her very differently, as did many others, I'm sure.

We tend to compare ourselves to other people. It's interesting to note that what we compare is what we value in others. So, if you compare yourself to someone who has a better job than you, it suggests that you value their type of job.

We also often see ourselves very differently from how others see us. Has someone ever paid you a sincere compliment about something that you were wearing and you thought, 'Oh, this old thing?' There is only one appropriate response to a compliment: smile and say thank you. If it's in your nature to explain or contradict the compliments you receive, change that behaviour immediately. It's counterproductive and sends the wrong message.

Lack of self-worth can cause you to waste money on things in an attempt to feel better about yourself, or to place yourself in a similar position to the people you admire. You are unique – value that and dig deep into your soul to find peace and self-love. When you value yourself, you are less inclined to spend money on stuff to feel better or fit in. Be yourself and get comfortable in your own skin. Spend some time alone. Write down what you value in yourself, and what others value in you. Then, compare the differences or similarities. It could be very insightful!

A word of caution, though: be careful of falling into the trap of 'if'. I've encountered women who believe that if they lost weight or got that new job, things would get better. Deal in reality – you can only work with what is here today. Consciously work at valuing yourself as you are now and the role you already play in your family, your community and your professional life. Valuing and loving yourself automatically takes you closer to your designer life. It makes you comfortable and confident in your own skin, and you stop wasting money and energy trying to be someone else.

3. Fill your own cup first

It's time to get a little selfish! Filling your own cup first is a simple concept, based on the idea that if your needs are met, you can meet the needs of others. It's a principle that can be applied in many situations, and one that springs to my mind is a family affected by addiction. Addiction can poison the entire family. All energy goes into trying to make the addict see the error of their ways. It's a horrible, taxing situation. It can make you feel helpless, as if you are on a merry-go-round of repeating behaviour. The real turnaround often happens when the addict's family members shift their focus to their own needs, instead of focusing entirely on the addict.

Many women don't have to deal with anything as difficult or traumatic as addiction, but we tend bear the burden of caring for others in our daily lives. As young girls, many of us were given dolls to play with, whereas little boys were given Lego and Meccano sets. We're taught to nurture others from childhood, and this implies putting our own needs on the back burner to prioritise theirs.

We cannot deny our nurturing side, but we need to acknowledge that we have our own needs and should consciously work on meeting them. It's easy to end up with feelings of resentment otherwise. Take a step back and identify what you need from a situation, on a physical, emotional, financial or spiritual level. Often, we know what we need in our gut, but are too scared to pursue it in case we offend someone or make them feel less important. A very wise therapist once told me that, if you don't stipulate your needs early in a relationship, the discomfort you feel just gets worse over time. It's better to stipulate your needs and boundaries upfront. The same is true of any other situation. Identify what you need, put it out there and work towards achieving it.

From a financial perspective, your most basic need is financial security. Let your actions ensure that. Prioritise growing your long-term wealth, which will provide you with that security. Pay yourself first, before you pay anyone else!

4. Set boundaries

Women are masters at juggling and pleasing people. Time is one of our most precious commodities in this rushed world, but we are bombarded with requests for our time, as well as our knowledge, our physical presence, or our emotional or financial support. Saying yes to every request can leave us exhausted and stressed.

Setting boundaries and learning to say no creates space, allows us some breathing room, and can ensure that we are giving in areas that add value to our lives. Boundaries are essential for a healthy life.

This may be easier said than done for many of us, but in situations where I need to draw a line, I love to apply the concept of 'no' being a full sentence. Over the years, I have learnt to become a little selfish in life, and the world is still turning. Some things that I have learnt:

- **Don't be afraid to be true to your needs.** In my corporate career I frequently travelled around the country, speaking at events two or three times a week. The travelling was gruelling and the impact on my family could be tough. I never found the juggling act of managing a career while raising kids as a single parent easy. It was particularly difficult to fly out on a Sunday and lose weekend time with my children, so I stopped speaking at events on Monday mornings or afternoons. That way, I could spend the whole of Sunday with my family. It was a small boundary, but it made a massive difference to my personal life.
- **Start small to gain confidence.** Once you see that your boundaries are respected, it becomes easier to set them.
- **Stick to your decision to set a boundary,** no matter how tempting it may be to give in. The worst thing you can do is set a boundary and then go back on your word. You won't be taken seriously next time. I know a young mother who stuck to her guns despite great temptation to give in. As a mom of two young children, she relished her bath time. It was her bit of relaxation and rejuvenation at the end of each hectic day. The family's home had only one bathroom, though, and every evening when she settled into the bath, one or both of her children insisted that they needed to use the toilet. Her quiet time was anything but quiet! She decided to set boundaries and locked the door once she was in the

bathroom. The first few nights, the kids wailed and howled on the other side of the door, but she refused to give in, as tough as it was. After a couple of days, all became peaceful. There were no more demands to use the toilet and her half-hour of tranquillity remained intact.
- **Be gentle but firm.** There is no need to get aggressive or defensive about setting boundaries. In fact, the best way is to be completely unemotional if you can.

When it comes to money, not setting boundaries can have devastating consequences, particularly if you feel you are being taken advantage of financially. It may be a family member who always needs a bit of help, or a partner who isn't pulling their weight financially. Be true to yourself and your needs, listen to your inner voice and remember that 'no' is a full sentence!

5. Pamper yourself

We all desire and deserve a bit of self-care and pampering, but instead of making your me-time a shopping spree, look for other ways to recharge. Taking time out of your schedule to relax or spoil yourself is excellent for your mental health, and sometimes for your physical health, too. But even if we acknowledge the importance, how often do we take the initiative? We seem to wait for someone else to take the lead, as if we need external validation before rewarding ourselves for hard work. This waiting can lead to resentment when our expectations are not met. It's not fair to expect others to know what we want or feel we deserve.

While I am a great advocate for pampering oneself, I admit that it sometimes still takes reminding. It doesn't have to cost a fortune; it's about nurturing and being kind to yourself. I learnt a lesson years ago in this regard. I love fresh flowers so, for me, they are always a treat. For many years, I waited for a man to buy me flowers. That was how I was raised – to believe that men buy women flowers. It rarely happened, of course. How did I react? With resentment. I didn't verbalise my need; I just expected him to know that I would have loved to receive a bunch of flowers. After some years I discovered that I could actually buy them in the shops myself, and I started buying my own flowers. No more resentment!

There are many other examples of pampering. We all value different activities. It may be a regular facial, a lunch out with girlfriends, or even just a trip to the local nursery. Spoil yourself once in a while and add it as a budget expense if you have to, but remember that it shouldn't take priority over necessities such as living expenses and savings. It's all about balancing your budget (which we discuss in detail in Chapter 9) without neglecting yourself in the process.

6. Be aware of your energy

Energy is inside and around us. It comes at us from all angles. Life, by its very nature, is an energy force so powerful that we cannot stop it. The energy we exude is an indication of our mental health having a great impact on the personal brand or image that we present to the world. Our energy flows through our body language, our words and our actions, often without us realising it.

We've all encountered people who drain us emotionally. You might feel great until you spend time with someone who makes you feel grim. We've probably also all encountered people who seem negative all the time: every time you speak to them, they complain that life is unfair, their boss is driving them uphill, their kids are battling at school, their relationship is rocky, and so on. Life seems to be a constant grind for them. I believe in standing by my friends through tough times, but when it becomes a barrage of negativity, I sometimes want to walk away. I once read some excellent advice on this issue: 'Stay away from negative people. They have a problem for every solution!'

We also all know people who cheer us up. We feel better for being in their company, and we enjoy their positive energy. We cannot always be upbeat, but energy is like a mirror: what you give out reflects right back at you. As much as we want to avoid negativity being projected onto us, we need to be aware of the energy we project onto others.

Body language plays a big role, too. What kind of energy are you projecting through your non-verbal cues? It is said that folding your arms across your chest is a gesture of self-defence, with the arms creating a barrier. Avoiding eye contact could be a sign of discomfort or dishonesty, resulting in a negative form of energy. Be aware of the signals that you send out to others and adapt your behaviour when necessary.

Sometimes we may need to hide our state of mind and don a mask for a specific situation. This mask may end up affecting the way we feel, for the better. Let me illustrate this. Over the years, I have done several keynote speeches to audiences of varying sizes, and I've never had a 'bad' speech. I don't allow whatever is going on in my mind or in my life to affect the message I deliver when I stand in front of an audience. The mask goes on.

I've had to do keynotes at times of great personal stress and couldn't allow my state of mind to cloud the delivery of my message. Often, I felt better after delivering the talk because I was able to distract myself from my negative thoughts and received positive energy from the audience. You may not have the opportunity to stand in front of an audience, but the principle remains the same. Often, the distraction of working, attending meetings or interacting with other people switches negative energy around and you feed off positive interactions.

Don't share your negativity with the world. If you are glum, keep it to yourself. Focus on the positive aspects of your situation and your mood will soon lift. However, if the source of your negativity is deeply rooted in depression or trauma, it is best to seek professional help.

Projecting positive energy is a critical part of your designer life. When things go wrong, deal with the situation and move on. Create a space that people want to be in. Remember, you attract more bees with honey than with vinegar!

7. Find your passion

Finding your passion is perhaps the most difficult and elusive aspect of creating your designer life, yet finding your sense of purpose and your reason for being on this planet is a major contributor to good mental health. It leads to fulfilment, serenity and a great sense of achievement.

It can be a rocky road. Many of us choose a career path without giving it too much thought. After school, we study further or start working, and before we know it, we are on that treadmill, working to pay bills from month to month. Too many people seem to be unhappy in their jobs and can't wait for Friday to come around.

We grow as people, too. As we experience different aspects of life over time, we change, learn new things and learn about ourselves – the greatest discovery ever. We may find that what we did in our twenties is very different from what we want to do when we reach our thirties or forties.

Our parents often play an important role in our career choice. A while ago I met two women who wanted to follow a certain line of work when they left school but were discouraged from doing so by their parents. After two decades of working, they finally went back to their passions and are making a resounding success of it. One had started a florist business, and the other a gourmet cooking business. Both women are in their fifties! It just took a bit of courage and a huge amount of faith.

You may find your passion but be hesitant to follow it fully if it does not pay enough to sustain your lifestyle. I agree that you should be practical and can start small. While you are busy with the job that pays the bills, nurture your passion in the evenings or on weekends. That side hustle may grow to the point where you can quit your day job and make your passion your full-time job.

I have also heard women say that they are too busy to follow their passion. For me, it's a case of priorities: if something is important enough, you will find time for it. I wrote three books while I was employed full-time. The first, *Dealing in Death*, was written over a period of four months, working evenings and weekends. While I wouldn't advise anyone to try it, I was so driven to write the book that it was not a chore but rather something I became completely immersed in.

And that's another point – if you are following your passion, work becomes a joy. It is rare to experience a situation that provides a perfect match between what you do for a living and what you want to do with your life. It's all part of creating your designer life, and you can do it if you put your mind to it!

* * *

Drawn together, these seven elements will bring you closer to your designer life – the one you want, not the one that others say you should live. You may not get it right all at once. Take baby steps. Outline what you need to focus on and tackle issues one by one. Soon you will find yourself in a happier, more contented space where you are not driven by other people or society's agenda. You will gain a clearer view of your life and purpose. You'll stop wasting money and start consciously building your wealth so that you can end up rich!

Chapter 7

Money and marriage

*'Money may not buy love, but fighting about
it will bankrupt your relationship.'*

– Michelle Singletary

For richer, for poorer; for better, for worse. Whether getting married is on your bucket list or not, have you considered the financial impact of this life-changing event? There is nothing more memorable than meeting The One, and then taking the enormous step to move in together or get married. Emotions will run high as you plan a lifetime of happiness together. Did you know that it could make you wealthier in the long run? In 2005, Ohio State University conducted research among 9 000 people and found that those in long-term marriages had about twice as much wealth as single people. Being married makes financial sense.

Why, though? It's not that 'a man is a financial plan'. Rather, partnership enables couples to share household expenses and financial responsibilities, allowing them to build wealth faster. Also, if one partner focuses on household duties, it can allow the other partner to focus on their career.

So, being married or partnered can give you a financial advantage over your single sisters, but it is only one element of the complex world of growing wealth. In addition, if your personal money matters are not dealt with properly, they can become a major source of unhappiness in a relationship. When people marry or commit to each other, finances are often the last thing they want to discuss or consider. Yet this is a life-changing step that can greatly affect your financial goals, dreams and aspirations. Understanding this and making sure that you discuss and plan things openly and together, can play a major role in creating and growing your wealth.

Weddings can be extremely expensive. Today, many couples pay for their own weddings or a substantial part of them. It's always good to consider exactly what you can afford, and what else you could do with the money if you made the wedding smaller or less elaborate. You and your partner need to discuss this carefully and consider all the options before making a final decision. It may feel like the most important day in your life, but you are also planning to spend the rest of that life together, so make the right financial decisions from the beginning of the journey.

Maybe it's your second time around. Or his. And maybe there are children and the two of you are about to discover the challenges of being a blended family. There may be financial commitments linked to previous relationships that will also play a role in your new life together.

But even if it's the first time for both of you, it doesn't make it any easier from a financial perspective. You might have different approaches to money, and it's wise to discuss this matter early on.

Money issues are a significant cause of stress in many relationships. In a 2015 survey of couples, SunTrust Bank in Georgia, United States, concluded that finances are the leading cause of stress in relationships. Of all the respondents who were experiencing relationship stress at that time, 35% said that money was the primary cause of friction. Interestingly, annoying habits came in second place, at 25%.

This is echoed by Relationships Australia, a leading provider of relationship support services in Australia. They found that 70% of couples experience tension over money issues at some point, and that this is a far stronger predictor of divorce than any other issue within a marriage.

Apart from money issues causing stress in relationships, the way in which you are married has vast financial implications, which many people do not consider at all. A marriage (between a man and a woman) or civil union (between same-sex partners) is a contractual agreement between two people. Stripped of all the emotions that come into play, it boils down to what is in writing (and what is not). This becomes crucial if the relationship ends. The terms and conditions of the agreement (the contract) dictate the division of assets. No one enters into a marriage or civil union thinking about divorce, but being smart means protecting your interests at all times. No one can predict the future.

For ease of reference, I will refer to marriages in this book, but the laws and principles apply equally to civil unions.

If no antenuptial contract is entered into before the marriage, the couple is deemed to be married in community of property. This has certain implications. By default, the bulk of marriages in South Africa are in community of property. A thorough understanding of your options and making the right decisions for your marriage contract are critical to your financial well-being.

If you do not want to be married in community of property, you need to draw up an antenuptial contract, specifying that you are married out of community of property. There is an additional option: your contract can include or exclude accrual. Let's examine the different options and their implications.

MARRYING IN COMMUNITY OF PROPERTY

When marrying in community of property, all assets and liabilities are combined, so both parties jointly own these assets and liabilities. Everything you and your partner owned (or owed) prior to the marriage is incorporated into the joint estate, excluding any items you have inherited. If your partner had debt before your marriage, you could find yourself responsible for paying it. Neither party can enter into a credit agreement without the other's permission. If your partner runs up debt while you are married, you are jointly responsible.

As everything is jointly owned, one partner cannot dispose of any assets (such as property or jewellery) without the written consent of the other partner. You will not need permission to sell an asset such as your car.

Both partners share in the profit and loss of the joint estate. Upon divorce, each partner will get half of the shared assets. So, even if you worked really hard during your marriage to accumulate assets, you would only be entitled to half of these upon divorce.

At death, you can only bequeath your half share of the joint estate. If you leave your share of fixed property to your partner, they would need to pay transfer fees to have it transferred to their name. This affects estate planning and liquidity.

MARRYING OUT OF COMMUNITY OF PROPERTY

Marriage out of community of property has two options: with the accrual system and without the accrual system. The antenuptial contract into which you enter before the marriage date specifies these details. The accrual system protects a financially vulnerable partner. When there is no accrual, each partner can manage their own assets freely.

Out of community of property with accrual

In the accrual system, whatever you bring into the marriage remains yours, and growth in the estate is jointly owned. The value of the estate and individually owned assets must be determined at the date of marriage. Certain assets can be excluded from the accrual in terms of the marriage contract and, in terms of the Matrimonial Property Act, any inheritance received and donations made between the parties during the marriage are excluded.

Under this marital regime, you are not responsible for your partner's debt, you can freely manage and grow your assets without your partner's permission, and any assets that you owned prior to the marriage are protected. If one partner decides to take time off work to raise the children, they are protected financially, as the accrued estate remains jointly owned. But for the partner who is financially stronger, sharing the assets that they worked so hard to accumulate could be a bitter pill to swallow.

Out of community of property without accrual

In the system without accrual, the assets owned prior to the marriage and all the assets accumulated during the marriage belong to the person who accumulated them. Nothing is shared and there is no joint estate. The same rule applies to liabilities – each person's debt is their own responsibility, and they may bequeath their assets upon their death as they wish.

The advantage of this system is that you control your own assets and can operate independently from your spouse. The disadvantage is that if you decided to take a career break to raise a family, you would have no financial protection in the case of divorce, as your spouse is not required to share any assets with you.

HE SAID, SHE SAID

Once you have decided which marital contract is best for you, the smart thing to do is to consider the differences that may exist in your approaches to money and how this will affect your relationship. You are both unique people with different personalities, likes and dislikes. You may be quite similar in certain respects, but vastly different in others – a case of opposites attracting.

It's good to have differences – life would be boring otherwise – but don't leave financial issues to chance. Have a frank discussion early in your relationship and try to understand each other's perspective of and attitude to money. One of you may be more conservative and the other more impulsive. Invariably, each partner believes that their approach is right and will behave in a way they deem to be correct.

There is no right or wrong approach, but there is the reality of two people under one roof. Some couples shy away from discussing finances, as it makes them feel uncomfortable. This may be a major flaw in their relationship, and love does not conquer all. Once the moonshine and roses fade and reality sets in, small differences can become huge issues that place undue stress on a relationship.

So, although talking about money upfront may feel uncomfortable, you might regret not having done so if you do end up fighting over financial issues. I think it's wise and can do no harm. Just as you would discuss your feelings about starting a family, your dreams and aspirations, and your approaches to raising kids, so should you discuss money – how you view it and how you plan to jointly manage your household expenses.

A relationship is based on honesty and transparency. It's also based on curiosity about your partner. What makes them tick? What do they like?

Or dislike? Favourite foods, favourite movies, best childhood experiences – the list is endless. Let this curiosity extend to their attitude to money. It can also be useful to determine how their parents treat money and what kind of example they set. A woman may have seen her father being the dominant money personality in the household and therefore anticipated taking a back seat in financial decisions. Meanwhile, her partner may have seen the opposite, and so expects her to take a more active role. Not discussing this openly could lead to rifts and misunderstandings.

Coupled with this, you need to know what your partner is bringing into the relationship or marriage apart from their fantastic personality. This includes debt, bad money habits or financial commitments over which they have no control.

A friend of mine fell in love with someone he considered an amazing woman. They got on like a house on fire. In addition to seeming like a good match for him, she was always well groomed and well dressed, a trait he found very attractive. Once they were married, however, an avalanche of window envelopes started arriving in the post – final demands for clothing-account payments, all addressed to his new wife. Initially, he just handed the envelopes to her, but when the sheriff of the court started delivering summonses, he sat her down. It turned out that she had reckless spending habits and that her debt had started piling up before they were married. In tears, she explained that she received her salary on the 15th of each month, but the accounts were due at the end of each month, by which point she had always spent all her money. He was shocked. The double whammy was that they were married in community of property, so he shared the responsibility for all the debt she had brought into their marriage, plus what she had incurred since then. It was a rude awakening: she took great care of her appearance, but he ended up paying the price. Sadly, the marriage didn't last.

We often take our cues from our parents, as mentioned in Chapter 3. If children are not taught to take responsibility for their spending and their parents are always willing to bail them out of tight financial spots, they could develop a 'someone-will-rescue-me' mentality and end up being unable to use credit responsibly.

On the subject of spending, damaging your partner's credit record is one of the biggest deal-breakers in a relationship. Running up debt for which your partner will be liable, or being driven by materialism in the form of wanting to spend money on expensive furnishings, a better house or a fancier car, for example, can be fatal for a relationship. When one partner encourages the other to go into debt for material things, but material things are not a priority for both partners, this could lead to resentment. The partners may then need to take on more than one job just to keep their heads above water, which could lead to burnout, as they never have time for important things such as relaxation, self-reflection and family. Your focus should be on the relationship, and happiness should come from other sources, not material possessions.

A relationship should be based on honesty. If one partner hides their debt or poor spending behaviour, this can be very damaging. Poor financial decisions could lead to shame, fear and isolation, which is unhealthy for both individuals and relationships. Even if the partner who is in debt manages to get themselves out of debt without the other partner's knowledge, it will still affect the relationship and detract from the financial goals the couple have set together. The risk, of course, is that everything comes out eventually; it usually does. By then, the problem may be enormous and could damage the relationship permanently.

The term 'financial infidelity' relates to a partner hiding their spending or deliberately deceiving their partner when it comes to finances. Keeping secrets from each other can damage the core of the relationship, namely trust. It can include behaviour such as:

- keeping a secret stash of money;
- incurring debt;
- earning money without telling your partner;
- spending money secretly on activities such as gambling, or buying big-ticket items;
- having a secret bank account; and
- selling assets without discussion.

How do you know if something is amiss? You know your partner well, and generally if their behaviour changes and your gut tells you that something is wrong, you're probably right. Red flags could include your partner suddenly becoming worried about your financial future, avoiding discussions about money, or being emotional or defensive when discussing money.

This is a difficult situation to deal with and couples may need professional intervention, as the root cause may be related to deeper problems in the relationship, such as a lack of self-esteem or control. These should be addressed before the damage becomes irreparable. Couples will need to address the situation in a non-confrontational manner. Admitting to each other that there is a problem is the first step. Both partners will also need to commit to finding a solution and moving forward together.

WHO WEARS THE PANTS?

Speaking of money and control: ego can raise its nasty head when one partner earns more than the other. This partner may fall into the trap of thinking they have more say in the relationship because they earn more. The classic situation is the homemaker who earns nothing, while their partner earns the income. Although the homemaker may be financially dependent on the breadwinner, this does not mean their position is inferior. Contributions towards a relationship or marriage entail much more than financial contributions: the financially dependent partner will bring her strengths to the party, while the breadwinner will bring money (and hopefully other strengths too!). If the relationship is built on trust and love, both partners will treat each other as equals, and their contributions will be seen to carry equal weight.

I have been asked several times what a homemaker can do to ensure her financial security. My answer is always the same – let your partner invest money for you, in your name, to give you some financial security.

Smartwomen never leave things to chance. Their understanding of their partners' approach to money enables them to anticipate conflict. This gives them a good chance of resolving issues in a mature way. So, discuss practical money issues openly. Do the following, in particular:

- **Decide how expenses will be paid.** Will you each take responsibility for paying for specific items and have a joint fund for expenses such as groceries, or will you simply divide all the expenses? Consider, also, that not everything has to be split 50/50 – the partner who earns more could pay a proportionately larger share.
- **Choose between pooled funds or individual payments.** Will you have a joint bank account for household expenses, or will each partner pay for certain items? I do not believe in a blanket joint bank account into which both partners' salaries are paid, as this gives you very little control over your money and can leave you vulnerable to your partner's spending habits. If one partner dies, the joint bank account will be frozen, along with all the other assets. This leaves the family in a difficult situation. I must add, though, that this is not cast in stone. I know a wealthy couple who have been married for nearly 40 years and had a joint bank account from day one. Their approach is simple: it's a business as well as a relationship, and they are both equal partners. So it can work, but only if both partners have common goals and the relationship is solid.
- **Decide who will manage the household finances.** Will you do so jointly? One partner is often better at managing the household finances than the other, which has nothing to do with how much either partner earns.
- **Draw up a household budget to which you both agree.** This should include: your non-negotiable necessities, such as bond or rent repayments, rates, insurance, car repayments, and loan or credit card payments; your variable necessities, such as groceries and clothing; and, finally, your discretionary expenses, such as eating out and entertainment, as well as your emergency fund (and even a home maintenance fund, if you own your home).
- **Set common financial goals** that address what you want to achieve and by when. If you agree with these goals, you will both be committed to them. You can start by listing your own goals and then sharing them with each other to find common ground.

A word of caution: couples sometimes fall into a spending pattern in which the woman spends her money on household expenses (furnishings, school fees, groceries, domestic help, and so on), while the man handles the bond, car and investment payments. This can leave a woman with very little to show for all her years of contributing to the marriage – and in a vulnerable position if she is not married in community of property.

MAKE PLANNING A PRIORITY

Your plan to grow your wealth needs to remain in your own hands, and getting married doesn't mean handing the reins to someone else. Continue with your investments and planning, as your partner will with theirs.

There will be common ground, though, and you will need to plan for joint goals and interests too. Your financial planning will therefore take place on two levels: joint interests and individual goals. Joint interests include the household and the family that you have together.

A will is obviously critical. You can have a joint will drawn up, which covers one or both of your deaths. Remember that the type of marriage or civil union into which you have entered will affect which assets you can bequeath upon your death. Remember, too, that minor children from a previous relationship are entitled to claim for maintenance against the estate until they are self-sufficient. This claim ranks above all other claims, with the exception of debt. Claims by other heirs are considered only after the maintenance claim has been paid. The smart thing to do is to make sure that the partner who has commitments from a previous relationship has sufficient life cover, so that their dependants or children are covered financially in the event of their death.

Another important consideration is the family's lifestyle, particularly if you have children. Most households require two incomes to maintain the family's standard of living. If something happens to one of the earners (death, disability or severe illness), and no provision is in place to cover it, you will have to draw from your investments. This will deplete your wealth, moving you in the opposite direction. So, it is important to protect your wealth as well. Otherwise, a family crisis could undo all the good you did up to that point.

Retirement planning is the ultimate reason to invest. Again, both partners should have their own retirement plan. Joint plans leave you vulnerable, as they may not materialise if something happens before you reach retirement age (one person dies, is retrenched or falls ill, or you get divorced). You both need your own portable retirement fund to invest in together, for your golden years. (We discuss retirement planning in more detail in Chapter 13.)

Nothing in life happens in a vacuum. We are surrounded and influenced by people and circumstances. Meeting that special person and settling down is all part of the process. If you handle it correctly, it can enhance your wealth tremendously. It's all about being smart – having the right approach and making wise decisions so that you can secure your future while enjoying every minute of today.

Chapter 8

The devastation of divorce

> 'Life is very interesting ... in the end, some of your greatest pains become your greatest strengths.'
>
> – *Drew Barrymore*

Remember the princess who kissed a frog and he turned into Prince Charming? And they lived happily ever after? Well, sometimes you marry a prince who turns into a frog!

Divorce is a reality for millions of South Africans. It's never part of the plan, but when it knocks on the door, there's no way of avoiding it. Divorce can have a significant impact on long-term wealth. I have often compared couples who stayed married with those who got divorced. Divorcees take huge financial knocks and often have their wealth and assets severely eroded. This appears to be backed up by solid research: the same Ohio State University research I mentioned in Chapter 7 found that individuals who had been married for a long time were far wealthier than their single counterparts.

This research also found that, when people get divorced, their wealth drops by an average 77%! This drop starts about four years before the divorce is finalised, and is probably due to the fact that people often separate long before the paperwork is done.

Jay Zagorsky, research scientist at the Center for Human Resource Research at Ohio State University, says, 'If you really want to increase your wealth, get married and stay married. On the other hand, divorce can devastate your wealth.' Of course, that is a hugely tongue-in-cheek statement! Staying married makes financial sense, but we all know this is usually not enough to keep two people together.

In South Africa, about one in three marriages end in divorce, often with devastating emotional and financial consequences. Assets are squabbled over as one future suddenly becomes two. Families are torn apart, and everyone has to reinvent themselves to start afresh. Divorce may be a new beginning, but it often requires a walk through hellfire to get there. It is one of the most stressful situations you can go through, particularly if young children are involved.

Most women get custody of minor children, placing them under additional financial strain. It is estimated that divorced mothers need to increase their income by about 30% to maintain their standard of living. Men, of course, need to pay child support, and sometimes alimony, so they also take additional financial strain while trying to maintain a home for themselves.

Irrespective of your marital contract, divorce will have a negative effect on your pocket. Even if you had your own investments and had built up your assets within your marriage, your ability to keep investing may be severely compromised, and you may find yourself having to dip into your capital to make ends meet.

Divorce is usually a lengthy process, and I would never wish it on anyone. But divorcees need to make smart decisions that will benefit them in the long run. Be wary of wasting money on the process itself. Once the divorce is under way, the knives are drawn, and the fight for assets and power commences. Even if there is a clear antenuptial contract in place, you still need to decide which assets belong to whom and how things will be allocated. Everything that forms part of your union, down to the smallest teaspoon, needs to be divided. This is no easy task, and divorce seldom happens without a squabble over the spoils.

I have heard divorced men say, 'I walked out with only the clothes on my back and left her everything.' I'm sceptical when I hear this. I think it could be an excuse for them having had little to start off with, and their ex-wives perhaps paid for the lion's share of the accumulated assets during the marriage. So the ex-wife was either legally entitled to them, or he let her have them out of moral obligation or guilt.

Whatever the circumstances, many see it as that one chance to take what they can – after all, they would otherwise have to start a new life without those resources. Both sides play games and make demands, and it's easy to waste money on these games. Divorce brings out the worst in people; I've even seen a situation in which a couple who were still living under the same roof communicated with each other about the terms of the divorce through costly lawyers' letters!

The bottom line is that no divorce can be settled unless there is agreement regarding assets and liabilities, as well as custody and child support if there are children. Attorneys charge handsome fees for facilitating this process; the more issues you dispute, the longer the divorce will take, and the higher your costs will be. The quickest and most cost-effective way of getting divorced is to reach an agreement as soon as possible. However, with emotions running high, people can get sucked into the battle, which can become a case of trying to outwit the other party. Sadly, this haggling can cost enormous amounts of money. The only ones who benefit from it are the attorneys. Any money wasted in the divorce process affects both parties, as there will be less to share afterwards.

You could, perhaps, consider using a mediator to assist you in reaching an agreement. This will be a lot cheaper than the cat-and-mouse game in which attorneys get rich. Even if your spouse is paying all the legal fees, any money they lose in this process means less for you and your children at the end of it. In trying to spite them by running up massive legal costs you will only spite yourself. You must reach an agreement eventually, so do it as cost-effectively as possible. It will benefit both of you.

GETTING YOUR FAIR SHARE

Your marital contract will determine how your assets are divided upon divorce, but after years of marriage not all ownership is clear-cut.

Before you draw up an agreement, it is useful to make a list of all your assets so that you can determine what belongs to whom. Bertus Preller, family law specialist and author of *Everyone's Guide to Divorce and Separation*, recommends gathering a list of each spouse's assets and liabilities, detailed monthly expenses, proof of each spouse's earnings, bank or credit card statements, mortgage bond documents or title deeds, pension or provident fund statements, and copies of any short-term insurance contracts that would list the value of these assets.

Any preparation work you do yourself will save you money in the long run. This is obviously much easier to do if you are working together to reach an amicable agreement, but most divorces aren't so easy. People may try to plead poverty or hide assets. They may undervalue their assets, set up a trust and transfer money into that, repay fake loans to family or friends, or fail to disclose bank accounts. I even heard of a man who ploughed large amounts of cash into casino chips as his divorce was pending. Once the dust had settled, he cashed them in again. I'm not sure if this story could be true, as I don't know enough about the casino world, but it certainly struck me as ingenious!

If assets are being hidden and you are battling to identify everything, a forensic accountant or an appraiser may be a good resource. Your financial adviser needs to be part of every step of the process so that your financial interests, as well as your legal interests, are protected.

If you are married in community of property, your retirement provision forms part of the communal assets, and one spouse could be entitled to a portion of the other spouse's pension fund, provident fund, preservation fund or retirement annuity (RA). That spouse's share can be taken in cash. The recipient will then have to pay tax on this amount, or may transfer their share into an RA, preservation fund, pension fund or provident fund. It must be clearly stated in the divorce order that the spouse who is not the member of the fund is entitled to a pension interest, as defined in the Divorce Act. This 'clean-break' principle means that the funds will be paid out within 60 days, and the spouse who is the member of the pension or provident fund will experience a significant drop in their retirement provision.

If you receive a portion of your spouse's retirement benefits upon divorce, you may be tempted to take the cash and spend it. This is not wise, as this money was to have formed part of the long-term wealth you were creating with your partner. You need to preserve it to continue growing this wealth. If you are the spouse who loses part of your retirement savings at divorce, you now have a serious shortfall in your retirement provision and need to ramp up your investments to make up for this loss.

KEEPING YOUR CHILDREN SECURE
If your divorce settlement includes child support for minor children, you may want to consider protecting this income. A number of things could affect your children's financial well-being:
- Your ex-partner could pass away. Your minor children would have a claim against their estate, but your ex may have minor children from other relationships, resulting in all the children competing for the same pot of money.
- Your ex-partner may become disabled or lose their job and become unable to earn an income. You can't get blood out of a stone, so you would be pretty powerless if they stopped paying child support.

A sudden loss of child support could be devastating for your financial situation. Be proactive and suggest that your ex-partner take out life and disability insurance policies, and perhaps even one for retrenchment. This should form part of your divorce settlement: he pays the premiums, but the policy is yours. As the policy then forms part of your divorce decree, it is an order of the court and he will be compelled to pay the premium. If he stops paying premiums for whatever reason, you can continue paying and the cover would continue. The policy is yours, so you have control.

SEPARATING THE FINANCIAL STRANDS
You will need financial and legal advice throughout the divorce process. The importance of financial advice at the time of divorce is easily overlooked, with potentially devastating consequences.

If the family home is being sold as part of the divorce agreement, use this to your advantage. This may be heartbreaking and stressful, and having children makes it even more difficult. However, realise that this property is part of the joint wealth that you had in your marriage, which is now no longer in place.

If you receive proceeds from the sale of the property, use them wisely, either as a deposit on a home of your own (or buy cash if you can), or as an investment in rental property. A few years back, a client of mine received a cash component as part of her divorce settlement. It was not enough to buy the home she needed for herself and her two children, so she decided to rent, but she used the money as a healthy deposit to buy a smaller flat, which she rented out. Apart from the rental income she received for that flat (which covered her costs), the value of the property rose handsomely and will be a valuable nest egg when she reaches retirement.

Children are a major concern in a divorce. Avoid changing schools or cities if you can help it. This stressful time will be made worse by uprooting everyone. Avoid burdening your children with too much unnecessary information. You may be tempted to confide in them, slate your ex-partner in anger in front of them, or even transfer your fears and insecurities about the future onto them. They don't need to carry this burden. Seek support from your family and friends, and focus on being strong for your children and positive about the future.

The least disruptive option for you and the children is to remain living in the family home after the divorce. If you own half the residential property (either because you were married in community of property or had an antenuptial contract with accrual), you may consider paying your spouse for their share and transferring the property into your name. You would need to take out a home loan for the amount, and have cash to pay the transfer fees. This will erode some of your wealth, but paying off your own home makes far better financial sense than paying rent to a landlord.

REVIEW YOUR WILL AND OTHER IMPORTANT DOCUMENTS

You will need to revisit all other aspects that you executed jointly with your ex-partner, such as your will, financial planning, and so on.

In terms of South African law, you have three months from the date of divorce to amend your will. Any bequest to your ex-spouse that is stated in your will would be deemed cancelled if you were to die within three months of your divorce. If your will stated that all your assets will go to your ex-spouse upon your death and you died within three months of the divorce, they would receive nothing. These assets would go into your estate and be distributed to your heirs.

If you do not amend your will within three months of your divorce, then your ex-spouse will benefit as indicated in the will. Changing your will is therefore paramount! Also, don't forget to update the beneficiaries on your policies to reflect your new situation.

You may have done some joint financial planning with your partner when you were married. Now you'll need to take care of yourself. You'll need to preserve and continue to grow whichever assets you built up during your marriage. You may have been on your spouse's medical aid, and now need to find your own. Shop around to find the option that best suits your needs, and get quotes from various providers. I am a great believer in buying things for their core value. Extras such as gym memberships and movie tickets are worthless if the scheme does not cover your medical expenses. That's what you need it for; the other bells and whistles are merely distractions. You may also need to consider your own retirement plan and make provision for your children's education.

Divorce is tough, but it's also an opportunity for renewal. Whatever the reason for the divorce, you cannot move forward if you keep looking back. Being smart means looking ahead instead of dwelling on the past. Focus on the positive aspects – the fresh start, the new-found freedom and the end of whatever unhappiness you may have been experiencing.

Don't lose yourself in a spending frenzy to feel better. Use your money wisely. Never lose focus on growing your wealth. You may not be able to invest quite as much as you could before your divorce, but keep investing. Every little bit adds up.

Chapter 9

Take control

'Some people make enough, some people don't,
and it has nothing to do with their paycheck.'

– Janene Murphy

If you are not in control of your money, you will never be financially free. If your money controls you, because of debt, as we have discussed, or through other behaviour, you've lost before you've started. But being smart means that you take control and can make the right investment decisions to make your money work hard for you.

No matter your circumstances or stage of life, there are some universal principles when it comes to money. Follow these, and you will place yourself in the driver's seat on the road to creating wealth.

CREATING BALANCE BETWEEN TODAY AND TOMORROW

While we are living our lives, often at breakneck speed, it can be easy to forget that tomorrow is just around the corner. Although we seldom stop to think about it, the reality is that we do not have infinite resources. We need a healthy balance to ensure that we can both live for today and invest for tomorrow. Some people are too focused on one of those priorities: either they spend it all today, or they save everything for tomorrow.

Extremes are never healthy. I have a client whose parents had been married for many years. I met her shortly after her father passed away. For her entire married life, her mother had been a housewife and never had any domestic help. She raised three children while doing all her own housework, because her husband tightly controlled the purse strings. They lived a very humble life and seldom went on holiday. A hard life, my client felt, and her mother had borne the brunt of it.

When her father died, they were surprised to discover that he had been rather wealthy – he had a good few million rand stashed away. But her mother, now aged 84, was too old and frail to enjoy any of it. Her father's intense focus on saving for tomorrow was commendable but perhaps extreme. Neither he nor his wife had enjoyed any of the money. Life had been unduly difficult, as his focus had not been on enjoying life today, but rather on tomorrow – quite a sad story, actually.

On the other end of the scale are people with a live-for-today attitude. For them, life is about the now, and tomorrow will take care of itself. It may, but then again, it may not, and what a risk to take! You could live a great life but end up with very little in the end, and your life is only good as long as there is money. At the tail end of our long lives, when we are no longer able to earn an income, we will still need money. Where will it come from?

A few years ago I met a couple who brought this dilemma home to me rather vividly. At ages 60 and 66 respectively, they wanted to start saving for retirement. They were both employed and together they earned a really good income, but apart from a home and two cars that were paid off, they had no assets or savings, except for one small policy. They enjoyed a good quality of life and travelled overseas regularly. This was all good and well, as long as they kept earning a good income. However, they had made no provision for the future or the unexpected, and when COVID-19 hit, their income disappeared overnight. When I last spoke to them, they were looking to use the proceeds from their policy to start a new business venture. Imagine having to start again at age 70. Rather strike a balance between living the good life today (your designer life) and taking care of tomorrow's needs. It's the smartest thing you can do.

FAMILY MATTERS

In a perfect world, your money is yours to spend and no one has any say over this, but for many of us the situation is quite different, and it can arise at various stages of life.

The term 'black tax' is used to describe the financial support that young professionals provide to family members. Then there are others who form part of the 'sandwich generation' and find themselves caught between supporting either adult children still living at home or aging parents, or both. If everyone has their hand in your pocket, you will be left feeling like the family ATM.

Money is a limited resource. When other people's needs take priority, yours are placed on the back burner. Money you spend on others could have been used as building blocks for your own financial future, whether it's saving for a car or house. In the extreme, it prevents you from building up enough wealth for your own old age, leaving you reliant on your children and perpetuating the cycle. This could also place huge strain on a relationship, especially if your partner is not supportive of you spending large amounts of money on family members.

Debt can be an easy trap to fall into when you try to juggle everything, and it may take real courage and restraint not to go down that rabbit hole. It's important to give only what you can afford to give, so make a point of working out your budget and providing support only within your means. Set boundaries for your support and make sure that your siblings contribute too. If you are supporting a sibling, help them to do a course or get an education so that they can find a job and be financially free from you.

FACE YOUR FINANCIAL REALITIES

A key principle you must embrace is to live the life you can afford, as opposed to the one you would like to afford. Some people live by the motto 'fake it till you make it', which is all good and well if you are vying for a promotion at work and trying to show that you can handle the job. It's not a good idea when you are trying to portray an image way above your income level. Getting into debt to have the right car, clothes and possessions – to look the part – could see you being the best-dressed defendant in the insolvency court.

Apart from the pressures of society and our drive to be successful, many people are single parents. This can put a huge strain on your pocket and wreak havoc on your financial planning. However, it is important to be aware of your reality and adapt your plans to allow for your changed circumstances.

You can only ever spend what is coming in. Do not be fooled by your gross salary – there are many deductions, and you can only spend your take-home pay. As the Australian footballer Bill Earle said, 'If your outgo exceeds your income, then your upkeep will be your downfall.'

If you experience any financial crisis, such as retrenchment or uncontrollable debt, it is important to face up to this. Hiding your head in the sand like the proverbial ostrich will not work. You need to face your reality and take appropriate action.

BUDGET

Budgeting gives you a clear picture of what is coming in and where it's going. Once the process becomes a habit, you will be more conscious of your spending and be able to identify and eliminate money-wasters. These creep into our daily lives and often we don't even realise they are there. Knowing that you are monitoring and tracking your spending will give you a feeling of satisfaction and empowerment. It will also help you counter any stress you may feel about your financial issues. Most importantly, you will learn how to use your money effectively, because you will be balancing your spending today with your long-term goals for tomorrow.

The first step in budgeting is to understand the difference between needs and wants, and how this distinction affects your spending. We discussed the difference between needs and wants in Chapter 5. Your basic needs are a roof over your head, clothing, food, electricity, transport and anything else you can't get by without. Your future needs may include buying a house, starting a family or funding a comfortable retirement.

Cluttering our thoughts are our wants. Sometimes we confuse the two, but your wants might include going on a cruise, splashing out on an expensive car or buying a house in a better suburb. These are things we desire but can live without. Our spending must cover our needs first and foremost. Only then do we address the wants.

The next step is to draw up your budget. You can do this with pen and paper, in Excel, or online. A handy budget sheet has been included at the end of this chapter. Doing your budget is like taking a selfie of your finances. You can see exactly where you are and what you need to change to achieve your goals. Start by listing all your income sources, including your salary, any child support payments and all other funds you are receiving. Remember to list your take-home pay here, not your gross salary. Total up your income streams to find your monthly income.

Next, list all your expenses, bearing in mind that you will have different types of expenses:

- fixed expenses (amounts that stay the same every month). These include rent or bond repayments, insurance premiums, school fees, gym memberships and cellphone contracts;
- variable expenses (amounts that may change from month to month). These include food, rates, water and electricity, and transport.
- irregular expenses, such as entertainment, home maintenance and general emergencies.

If you have set long-term goals, budget for these under fixed expenses, provided that this is realistic. (We discuss goal setting in more detail in Chapter 11.) You may also want to pay off some debt, and can use your budget to track your progress.

Make sure that your income and expenses balance. If you are spending more than you earn, you clearly need to cut back somewhere.

This will be your planned budget. As you spend throughout the month, keep a record. Use an 'actual' column on your budgeting sheet to see where there were differences between what you anticipated and what you spent.

There are some excellent budgeting apps that can help you budget and track your expenditure, including 22seven, Goodbudget, Mint and Wallet. Some banking apps also do this, so see what additional features your banking app offers. Find and use the tools that work for you. You may need to adapt or change your budget as things happen. Perhaps you'll receive a salary increase, for example, or get a bonus in your birthday month or at year-end. Work these changes into your budget so that you use this money effectively – it's not just a windfall to be spent recklessly.

Smartwomen use the budgeting process as a tool to control their money and help them achieve their long-term goals. By budgeting and staying committed to your financial goals, you build your wealth and get rich over time.

PAY YOURSELF FIRST

Coupled with the budgeting exercise is the wonderful concept of paying yourself first. As payday draws near, everyone queues up for their share of your money. You will also have other commitments – groceries, petrol, clothing and a host of other expenses to fund your lifestyle.

If you are someone who receives a salary, pays the bills and other living expenses, and then hopes there will be something left to save, you will know that you seldom save anything, if ever. Many of us spend it all and wait in eager anticipation for the next salary.

To build wealth and get rich, you need to make saving a priority. When your creditors line up on payday for their share of the cake, place yourself in the very front of the queue. By paying yourself first, you prioritise yourself before anyone else. You are committed to your goals, working actively towards building your wealth.

Investment guru Warren Buffett, one of the richest men in the world, sums it up beautifully: 'Do not save what is left after spending, but spend what is left after saving.'

It may seem impossible for some people to pay themselves first when life is so expensive and there are so many bases to cover with their monthly salary. The point is that it is all about priorities. If it is your priority to build your wealth and get rich, then talk is cheap, but money will buy the whisky! You need to take action to achieve results. Being smart means making the goal of building wealth a priority and finding the money to do so. Shift things around in your budget to make it work. Your savings fund should be right at the top of the list. Work the rest of your expenses around it. People who pay investment and pension fund contributions via a stop order from their salary pay themselves first without having to think about it, so they can automatically only 'spend what is left after saving'.

LIVE OFF LAST YEAR'S INCREASE

Closely linked to paying yourself first is a nifty trick that will allow you to accumulate vast wealth by making one small change in your life: decide to not take your salary increase one year and invest this money instead. When the next year comes along, take last year's salary increase only, and invest your current increase. Repeat this every year, so that you are constantly living off last year's increase and investing your current increase.

Let's look at an example to make this clearer. For the sake of simplicity, we will ignore income tax and the impact of inflation.

- Pumla is 25 years old and earns R20 000 per month. She receives an increase of 6% every year and invests it at a return of 12%.
- In year 1, she receives an increase of R1 200 and invests this. Her salary is now R21 200, but she lives off R20 000.
- In year 2, she receives an increase of R1 272 and invests this. Her salary is now R22 472, but she lives off R21 200.
- In year 3, she receives an increase of R1 348 and invests this. Her salary is now R23 820, but she lives off R22 472.
- In year 4, she receives an increase of R1 429 and invests this. Her salary is now R25 249, but she lives off R23 820.
- In year 5, she receives an increase of R1 514 and invests this. Her salary is now R26 764, but she lives off R25 249.

She maintains this pattern every year and, at a growth rate of 12% average per annum, manages to accumulate a lump sum as follows:
- at age 40 (after 15 years): R785 652
- at age 50 (after 25 years): R3 244 783
- at age 55 (after 30 years): R6 183 180.

One small change and look what she manages to accumulate! That's being in control. The only sacrifice she made was her salary increase in the first year. She received an increase each year thereafter – it was just the previous year's increase. Put another way, all she did was take her very first salary increase and invest it, increasing it by 6% each year.

Assumptions have been used here to illustrate the point. These include that the interest rate remains the same and that Pumla does not get a promotion or earn a better salary. If she gets promoted or gets a job with a better salary, she will be in an even stronger position to invest more and catapult herself to a position of wealth. It's all about choices; being smart keeps you moving forward on the road to riches.

ELIMINATE MONEY-WASTERS

Your budget should give you great insight into where your money is going, but have you ever considered those hidden expenses you are probably unaware of? I have always believed that if you don't know about something, then you probably don't need it. I call these things money-wasters – things you can stop spending money on, with little or no impact on your lifestyle.

Here are some to consider:
- **Subscription services:** It may feel great to get your newspaper or magazine delivered to you, but do you actually read it? It's easy to read the latest news online, and many people simply don't have the time or inclination to sit and read a newspaper cover to cover. So, get your news for free and buy magazines only when you really want them – not just because they are there.
- **Designer brands:** There is little justification for designer items costing what they do, but because they cost more, they are perceived to be of better quality. And, of course, a designer brand is a status symbol. I believe that every woman can look well-dressed by knowing how to dress. It's not about the label but about how you plan your wardrobe, combine items and develop your own personal style. Do some research online or consult a wardrobe planner if you need help, and learn how to look fabulous every day by mixing and matching cleverly instead of

spending a fortune on clothes. This is a frequent money-waster for some women!

- **Make-up:** In the past, I spent hundreds (if not thousands) of rands buying make-up and trying different foundations in the quest to find the perfect colour for my skin. It was a terrible waste of money, until I went for a professional foundation matching. It is well worth the investment, as is a good make-up lesson or two. You can achieve a professional look with a few high-quality products and save thousands by no longer buying products to experiment with at home, hoping to get it right.
- **The latest gadgets:** Just when you think you have the latest gimmick, a new one comes along. It's almost impossible to keep up. Rapid advancements in technology tempt us to have the latest gadgets so we do not fall behind. We are judged by how tech-savvy we are, and it's really not cool to be old school. As an added pressure, many people today feel the need to be connected all the time. And how many people end up stressed and burnt out? We never seem able to switch off. Don't fall into this trap. Use your gadgets for the needs you have, not for the needs the manufacturer says you should have. Understand what the gadget can do, and buy it only if it has value to you. Keep it simple and cost-effective.
- **Gym membership:** If you use yours, great. But many people get suckered into taking out a membership because of an alluring offer or because they genuinely believe that they will use it. If your commitment has waned and you are only keeping your membership in case you may start using it again, cancel it. Jogging around your neighbourhood is free.
- **Vitamin pills:** Increasingly, scientists are proving through research that vitamin pills have few or no health benefits. A balanced diet provides all the nutrition you need to be healthy.
- **Bank charges:** Shop around for the best deal. Don't get caught up in the status of a more prestigious banking product with shinier cards. My bank has approached me more than once to upgrade to a 'better' banking package. It costs close to double what I am paying now, and all I get is a smarter credit card and a personal banker. What do I need that for? My simple account package meets all my needs.

- **Bottled water:** Aside from bottled water being expensive, producing and shipping the plastic bottles – most of which end up on the rubbish dump – uses valuable resources. It's bad for your pocket and even worse for the environment. The water in our taps is perfectly safe and virtually free.
- **The daily takeaway coffee:** At about R25 a cup, you could save about R550 per month. Make your own, put it in a small flask and use the money you save for something better.
- **Lotto tickets:** Your chances of winning the lottery are about one in thirteen million, yet people still religiously spend money on Lotto tickets. This is clearly not a way to get rich. Rather invest this money and watch it grow.
- **Policies:** Check what you are paying for in terms of your policies. Get proper advice and make the effort to understand exactly which benefits you will receive. I sometimes encounter people who have been sold far too much life cover, or duplicate types of cover. Cut out what you don't need and find a reliable financial adviser who can assist you.
- **Car insurance:** Shop around for the best deal. Your car decreases in value each year, so make sure that your premiums reflect this. Review your car insurance regularly and get quotes annually to see if you are still getting the best deal.
- **Home entertainment:** If you have DStv, pay for this service annually in advance and save one month's subscription fee. Perhaps you can also consider downgrading to a cheaper package that still suits your needs. I know of people who use the full DStv package only during the school holidays and have a cheaper option for the rest of the year. An alternative is to switch to one of the many streaming packages that offer endless entertainment at a more affordable cost.
- **School fees:** Some schools offer a discount if you pay the full annual fee upfront. Find out which options are available.
- **Debt:** This is arguably the biggest money-waster of them all. The interest you pay on debt is money flushed down the drain. It's such a big issue that I've examined it in a chapter of its own (see Chapter 10).

- **Grocery shopping:** Cut back on your bill by leaving the kids at home. You won't be tempted to overspend. Also don't shop when you're tired or hungry. Always have a shopping list. Avoid the displays and all temptations to get you to impulse buy. Consider online shopping – you can track exactly what you're spending and there are fewer visual temptations to grab items you never intended to buy!

BUDGET SHEET

Use this handy budget sheet to get on track and stay in control of your money.

Income		Expenses – fixed	
Salary		Rent/home loan repayments	
Child support		Levies/rates and taxes	
Rental income		Security	
Commission		Policies and investments	
Bonus		Loan repayments	
Interest		Domestic help	
Other income		Medical cover	
		Insurance – car and household	
		School fees	
		Car repayments	
		Emergency fund	
		Home entertainment/Internet	
		Other fixed expenses	
		Expenses – variable	
		Toiletries and medicine	
		Telephone/cellphone	
		Groceries	
		Pet food and care	
		Petrol/transport	
		Electricity and water	

		Expenses – variable	
		Store card repayments	
		Credit card repayments	
		Educational expenses	
		Extramural activities/ pocket money	
		Clothing	
		Other variable expenses	
		Expenses – irregular	
		Books, magazines, music	
		Entertainment and hobbies	
Total income		**Total expenses**	
Income less expenses: surplus/shortfall			

Chapter 10

Dealing with debt

'Debt erases freedom more surely than anything else.'
— *Merryn Somerset Webb*

Being in debt is simply not smart. Sadly, many South Africans are drowning in it. It's very easy to slip into debt, but hugely difficult to get out of it, and it robs you of the ability to build wealth. The severe financial implications of COVID-19 have forced many people into debt just to survive. Others have had to rely on payment holidays on their existing credit arrangements to tide them over. Even before COVID-19, though, debt levels in South Africa were alarmingly high. For many years, people have succumbed to the allure of store cards, credit cards, overdrafts and personal loans, all of which are widely marketed and provide a false sense of wealth. Usually, they realise too late that all they have been achieving is a stream of repayments that never seem to end.

If you feel overwhelmed by debt, you are not alone. But we all deal with stress differently. Some people simply ignore their ever-increasing debt: they don't open the envelopes or emails as they arrive, as if it will all just go away. Others fall into a pit of depression, feel powerless and fear losing everything.

Debt can take a terrible toll on relationships: one partner might blame the other for their role in incurring the debt, not earning enough money to pay it off, or for losing their job and therefore their payment capacity. The old expression 'when poverty comes in the front door, love goes out the back door' is true; many divorces are rooted in financial problems.

Some people may feel resentment, subconsciously blaming their employers for not paying them enough. Or they may be angry with themselves for spending as they did and regret the decisions they made.

SPEND TODAY, PAY TOMORROW

When we incur debt, we use tomorrow's money to fund today. We are spending it now, hoping that we will have the means, in the future, to pay it back. For a number of reasons, though, it is easy for debt to spiral out of control. Credit is easy to access, although amendments to the National Credit Act in 2014 brought far more stringent requirements to bear for obtaining credit. They were aimed at providing consumers with greater protection against reckless credit providers.

For many people, though, these amendments were a case of too little, too late. Those who can service their debt might have realised what a waste of money debt is. It comes at a huge cost: the interest you pay is money you waste. You receive no benefit from paying this money, except the privilege of having access to funds or goods before you paid for them.

Not all debt can be considered the same, however. There is 'good' debt and 'bad' debt. It's the bad debt that often leaves us wondering what we actually got in return – store cards, credit cards, personal loans, and so on. This type of debt is often incurred to acquire goods and services that are not durable. Before you have even paid for that expensive meal, it has been digested!

By contrast, 'good debt' is debt incurred for the sake of an investment that will bring you future benefits or returns. When you use other people's money to create wealth for yourself – by buying a rental property using a loan from the bank, for example – you are incurring good debt. Purchasing a home to live in is a lifestyle investment that gives your family security, so the loan you take out to buy that home also counts as good debt. Student loans are also a form of good debt, as they allow people to invest in their future: the skills students acquire in their studies enhance their future earning potential.

A car is never an investment from a wealth-creation perspective, but most people would not be able to purchase a car without using credit.

A good car is an investment in your safety, so I classify it as good debt – as long as you make clever choices when buying a car, as discussed in Chapter 5.

PUPPET ON A STRING

Regardless of whether your debt levels are manageable, debt is costly and prevents you from building wealth. When you are in debt, you are not in control of your money, and your creditors can manipulate you like a puppet on a string. You are committed to paying them before you start paying yourself or your living expenses, never mind finding money to invest for tomorrow. You work for them, not for yourself. When you're in debt, your money is not working for you – you are working to make money that you have already spent.

DOWN WITH DEBT!

We all know people who have managed to get themselves knee-deep in debt. In fact, I often wonder how some people afford their lifestyles. Too many people build them on debt, and if that debt is not managed properly, they can drown in it. This was brought home to me rather sadly by a former colleague, who always joked, 'I have a great bank manager. If I need money, I just go and speak to him.' I thought this a strange perspective, but we never discussed it much. A year later, he lost his home.

You can only run so fast on the debt treadmill before it overwhelms you, so get off before it's too late. You have to face the situation and start digging yourself out of debt, while simultaneously implementing actions that will prevent you from going into more debt in future. If your situation is dire and you can no longer service your debts, it's time to come clean and face your creditors. Be honest and offer to pay back a smaller amount each month until the debt is redeemed. You can formalise this through a debt review process: you are declared over-indebted, and a debt counsellor negotiates a restructured payment plan with your creditors and obtains a court order confirming the new repayment plan.

Another option is debt consolidation. You can do this through a debt consolidation loan, where you take out one large loan, and pay back all your smaller debts. You can also increase your home loan if there is enough equity (value) in the property and use this money to settle your smaller debts. This may work wonders for improving your monthly cash flow, but a word of caution: debts are all repayable over a certain term, so be careful not to consolidate them and then pay them off over a longer term, because this will ultimately cost you more money. For example, suppose you have credit card and store card debt that you cannot repay. These debts were probably payable over 12 or 24 months. You could increase your home loan by this amount, settle your short-term debts and pay an increased home loan instalment, but the problem is that you still have, say, 15 years' worth of home loan to repay. Don't exchange short-term debt for long-term debt. Rather pay off the new loan amount over the same period – 12 or 24 months.

These are drastic options that you should use only as a last resort. If you want to tackle your debt more subtly, here are some simple steps you can follow:

- Make a list of all your debt, noting the outstanding balance, monthly repayment amount and interest rate. This will give you the big picture and help you make decisions about how to tackle it.
- Scrutinise each account to see exactly what you are being charged for every month. What other costs are being added? A common addition is credit life insurance, which is very expensive and covers you for death, disability and retrenchment, depending on the structure of the cover. It settles your account in full if you die, or are disabled or retrenched. This cover proved to be very useful when people were retrenched during 2020 at the height of the COVID-19 lockdown period in South Africa. Make sure that your cover is not duplicated – if you have sufficient life/disability or retrenchment cover elsewhere, contact the creditor and ask them to remove the credit life insurance. Be aware, too, that the cover may not apply to you.

In 2016, Lewis Stores was found to be in breach of the National Credit Act for selling loss of employment and disability cover to pensioners and unemployed people as part of credit insurance. Lewis Stores was ordered to refund customers the premiums they had been charged.

Clothing retailers often offer club membership, for which you may also be paying. Benefits of these clubs may include a magazine (that you don't need) and special discounts on purchases, meaning that you need to spend more money to save money! Remove it, and use that extra R40 or R50 a month for paying off your account. Every little bit helps! As consumers, we all need to be careful about granting permission for club membership or other additions to our accounts, so that we don't pay for something we do not need.

Contact your credit provider to see whether they can offer you a lower interest rate. It's not always wise to have financial products with different companies, as they often offer better rates if you keep everything under one roof. For example, you may get a better rate if your home loan and credit card are with the same bank. Do your homework on this.

Next, draw up a plan for eradicating your debt. List your debts from smallest to largest using the template on page 94, and pay them off as usual, but stop buying on the first account that you settle. Cut up the card and close the account so that you are not tempted to buy again. Someone once told me that her aunt would pay off an account and, once it had a zero balance, became so excited that she started spending on it again. Retailers are there to make money; a zero balance is not something they value. If your account is active but has a zero balance, they will send you all kinds of correspondence, discount coupons and gift vouchers to tempt you to spend again. Rather close the account. When you have completely settled one debt, move on to the next one on your list. Pay the instalment plus whatever you were paying on the first debt. Once this debt has been settled, move to the third one, following the same pattern. In this way, you will eliminate your debts methodically and bring your money under control. This is something referred to as the 'snowball' method of reducing debt, because you gain momentum as each debt is paid off. Remember, this process will not happen overnight – it probably took you months or years to get into debt, so getting out of it will also take time. Be patient and you will reap the benefits.

Reward yourself for paying off each debt. Buy or do something you value – but use cash! You will feel motivated and inspired when you start seeing your debt shrink.

Use windfalls such as your annual bonus (if you receive one) to make a dent in your debt. Do not use all this money for debt, though – keep some aside for spoiling yourself, or you may be tempted to go into debt again. It's a wonderful feeling to be flush with money, but use it wisely, so that it is not all consumed and lost in memory.

In conjunction with an active plan to reduce your debt, you may also want to look at your spending patterns and consider some innovative ways to boost your income.

SMARTER SPENDING

Start becoming conscious of your spending. We all know that feeling – you're out shopping, you spot some 'must-have' item and decide that you just have to buy it. Try giving yourself 24 hours to think about it. A good friend gave me this tip many years ago: whenever she found herself in a shop looking at a pair of shoes she wanted, she would tell herself that she would come back the next day to buy them if she really wanted them. Of course, she seldom went back the next day.

I have followed this advice many times, and I've never gone back to buy the item. Something else soon distracts you and you forget about that thing you thought was important. Impulse buying is a very powerful force, so be aware of it and put a plan of action in place to counter it.

Look at other areas, too, in which you could become smarter with your spending. Could you do your own nails instead of going for a manicure? What about packing lunch for work instead of buying lunch every day? Could you plan your meals a week in advance so that you shop for groceries more effectively – once a week, perhaps, which works out much cheaper?

Many of us spend money eating out or getting takeaways on a Friday night. For a family of four, this can easily amount to R500 or more. That's R2 000 per month just on Friday dinners! See if you can start a supper club with some friends, or get the family to buy into eating out every second Friday only, which will halve your eating-out expenses. Look for innovative ways to make this fun. Each family member could have a turn to cook the Friday meal (or one course of the meal), perhaps, and the other family members could rate it. The winner could receive a small prize: movie tickets or a gift voucher, or something relatively inexpensive. Or do it just for fun and family bonding.

Use loyalty cards where they are offered for free. Loyalty programmes are built into the prices of the goods or services you are already buying, so you may as well benefit from them. If you have to pay for a loyalty programme, do your homework carefully beforehand to see if it's worthwhile. How much would you need to spend to receive real benefits?

And, of course, don't forget that a vital tool for managing your spending and decreasing your debt is budgeting.

PAY OFF DEBT OR INVEST?

I am often asked which is better: paying off your debt first and then starting to invest, or investing while paying off debt. There's no one-size-fits-all answer. Logically, the interest you pay on your short-term debt will always be higher than the investment return you could earn, so it makes sense to pay off your debt first. When you consider longer-term debt – such as a home loan, which usually has lower interest rates – it is entirely possible to achieve higher returns than the interest you are paying, so you could be paying off a home loan and investing at the same time.

Interest rates have been rather low for quite some time, so the cost of borrowing may be cheaper, but then again, the return you earn on investments may be lower. Whether interest rates are high or low, it's all relative. At the time of writing, the home loan base rate is 7% per annum. If you have spare cash, you need to decide whether to pay it into your home loan or invest it. Some investments have delivered returns way above that percentage over the past five to ten years, so the smart decision may very well be to invest your extra cash instead of paying it into your home loan. You need to invest it in the right place, of course, so consider your situation carefully and seek advice.

Also remember to take tax into account. Paying money into your home loan has no tax implications, but investing will attract tax on interest, dividends and capital gain. The return earned on your investment may be diminished because of this.

Deciding where to invest spare cash is not easy, and you need to consider a number of factors, including your own level of discipline. If you pay extra money into your home loan, you may be tempted to dip into the loan (most banks have this facility). This could mean ending up, after 20 years, with an outstanding balance on a home loan and no investments. Make your decision based on your personal situation and review it regularly.

As a rough rule of thumb, eliminate short-term debt before you start investing. Commit to not incurring short-term debt again, and to starting an investment plan. If you are in any doubt about the correct route to follow, get advice. Often, someone objective can see things differently.

Reducing debt takes discipline and patience, as does investing for the long term. But the rewards are immense. The satisfaction and relief you will feel as the debt noose slips off your neck, and the joy of seeing your wealth growing, will be far more powerful than any pleasure you can derive from shopping. Learn from your mistakes so that you don't ever fall into that trap again, and commit to a smarter, better way of working with money.

DEBT BUSTING

List your debts from smallest to largest and start eliminating them! Use this table as a template, or set up your list in a spreadsheet program such as Excel to track your progress.

Creditor	Amount owed	Interest rate	Monthly repayment	Balance of repayment period	Total due

Chapter 11

Getting your hustle on

'Challenges are gifts that force us to search for a new center of gravity. Don't fight them. Just find a new way to stand.'

– Oprah Winfrey

If money is tight and it feels like there is no way out, remember that there are only two levers you can pull to change the situation – either spend less or earn more. If you are paying off a mountain of debt, have cut your spending to a minimum or you just want some extra money to spoil yourself, consider starting a side hustle.

As a result of the devastating impact of the recent pandemic, many people either lost their jobs or had to take a pay cut, so a side hustle became the only option. The numbers tell the story. A 2021 poll by ecommerce platform Gumtree revealed that over 30% of South Africans have a side hustle, or that this has become their main source of income. A further 46% were considering starting a side hustle.

If you're working full time for an employer, make sure that you are permitted to have a side job. Some employment contracts prohibit this, or it is only allowed if it is disclosed and the employer grants permission.

The easiest way to generate extra money is through a passive income – you initially put in the work, and then it makes money for you. Examples of this would include rental income from an investment property, royalties from writing a book, or investing in an existing business where you receive a share of the profits. For many of us, though, these are not viable options, so we need to actively work to generate that income.

GETTING STARTED

It may be daunting to decide what to do as a side hustle. If you have specific skills, you may want to offer these on a freelance basis, or you may want to start a brand-new business. Here are a few easy steps you can follow to refine your ideas:

Step 1: Brainstorm and list all the ideas you can come up with. Don't be put off by the fact that you may not be able to do the job or that you don't have the time – just list everything you can think of, based on the services that you use, and write down any other ideas you've picked up from the internet or your friends. You will trim the list as you go along.

Step 2: Identify things on the list that you would enjoy doing. You don't want to be spending your spare time on something you find painful.

Step 3: Find out if your idea services a need and whether people are prepared to pay for it. Would *you* pay for it? If so, how much? Do some research and see if anyone else offers the same product or service and what they charge. You may have a great idea, but if no one is prepared to pay for it, then ditch it.

Step 4: Get started on your idea. Advertise on social media and online market platforms such as Gumtree. Join networking groups or groups with similar interests. It will take you a while to build your reputation and to get new clients. Remember that referrals are the most powerful way to attract new clients.

SOME CASH-GENERATING IDEAS

Getting a side hustle going can be tough, especially if you are used to a clearly defined workday and a regular salary. Here are some ideas that you can consider to get started:

- **Tutoring:** If you have knowledge or skills in a certain area, tutoring can be a lucrative side hustle that takes only a few hours per week. You don't have to be a qualified teacher. Parents are happy to pay extra to

ensure that their kids thrive in school. Look at websites such as Indeed for job opportunities, or register with specific tutoring websites such as www.teachme2.com, www.turtlejar.co.za or www.superprof.co.za.
- **Sell on the side:** If you have a large network, perhaps through your church, community or workplace, consider selling products as a sideline. It gives you the flexibility to work when you want to, and the more effort you put in, the greater the potential reward. There are a wide variety of direct selling products, including Avon, Almay, Honey Jewellery, AMC Cookware and Inuka Cosmetics.
- **Dog walking or pet sitting:** If you love animals, this is a great way to generate some extra cash. You will need to be available over weekends and holiday periods, such as Christmas, when people go away and need their pets cared for. Advertise your services on Facebook or Gumtree. It may also be useful to sign up with a professional pet-sitting service, just to get started. There are many available; most are specific to a particular city, so Google is your best friend when trying to find a list of local pet-sitting or dog-walking services.
- **Housesitting:** In a similar vein, housesitting involves taking care of someone's home while they're away. This may include watering plants, overseeing repair work and sometimes even cleaning and grocery shopping before the owner's return, if required. It may or may not include pet sitting. It's an easy way to make money while still doing your full-time job. You can advertise your services locally or join one of the many agencies that operate in your area. Again, Google can assist.
- **Turn trash into cash:** The upcycling trend is huge and there is money to be made if you are good with your hands and can restore and revamp old furniture and items that would otherwise have been discarded. Outdated items can be beautifully transformed with a bit of creativity and elbow grease. There are many creative ideas on Pinterest and other sites (simply google 'upcycling'). With furniture, you'll need a bit of knowledge about what can be successfully restored and what is old junk, and you'll need a bit of cash to get started, but this really is a creative and fun way to make some extra money.

- **Give your opinion:** Online surveys can bring in a little extra money. You won't make a fortune, but how much time do we waste endlessly browsing through social media? That time could be spent doing surveys to make some money. There are a number of websites where you can register to do surveys. Just make sure you understand the payment; some pay with rewards or vouchers, while others pay cash once you have accumulated a certain level of earnings. Some sites to check out include www.triaba.com/za, www.springvaleonline.co.za and www.surveycompare.co.za.
- **Film or TV extra:** If your time is flexible, this is a great way to make some money with little effort. Films, series, TV commercials and stills often require people in the background so that scenes appear real and natural. They do not have speaking roles. Many different types of extras are needed, depending on the production. To get started you will need to get a good-quality headshot and register with one or more agencies. Do some research, as some agencies are area-specific, while others operate on a national level. Check out www.colttalent.com, www.mcx.co.za (Cape Town), and www.aardvarkcasting.com, to name a few.
- **Virtual assistant:** If you have the skill and ability to work remotely, you can market yourself to the many people who make use of freelance business services. These can include diary management, admin, social media management, writing, transcribing, or even basic accounting and payroll services. If you need to hone your skills or develop a new one, do a course on an online learning platform such as Udemy (www.udemy.com). There is also a Virtual Assistants Association for South Africa (www.vaasa.co.za); their website contains useful information about virtual work and allows you to register your services. Other virtual assistant agencies include www.outsourcery.co.za, www.vaconnect.co.za, and www.upwork.com.
- **Focus groups:** These formalised groups are used by research houses to ensure that a company's products meet the needs of their target audience, and to test whether the packaging and advertising are effective and accurate. Focus-group activities are generally conducted at their offices, but some may take place online. Look at www.opinionhero.com and www.thebrandsurgeon.co.za for more information.

- **Sell your images:** Put your photography skills to good use and make some money out of your images. Stock-image websites keep a wide variety of images, illustrations and video clips that are downloaded and used by designers for websites and other marketing material. Each time an image is used, the photographer is paid. The most popular images are those of people, nature, cities, food and travel. Check out www.stock.adobe.com, www.shutterstock.com and www.alamy.com as some options to get started.
- **Teach online:** There are a number of options, from teaching English online to teaching a specific skill that you have and can share with others. There is no limit to what you can teach online. Do you know how to sew? Can you play the piano? Do you know how to speed read? Teach others. Over 150 000 online courses are on offer at udemy.com, so it's a great place to start looking to get you motivated.
- **Get crafty:** If you're creative and love to make things, it may be your hobby, but how about turning it into a money-making opportunity? Handmade items are in huge demand, including clothing, home décor, art, bags and jewellery. These items can be sold via websites such as www.etsy.com or www.hellopretty.co.za, which specialise in handmade items. You could also open your own store on www.shopify.com or sell through Facebook Marketplace.
- **Money for jam:** TV, film, advertising and photographic location scouts are always on the lookout for suitable locations and often use private homes, commercial buildings and even gardens for this purpose. All types of properties are suitable – from sophisticated city dwellings to slightly dilapidated buildings. They pay well, as it's cheaper than building a set from scratch, so it's worth exploring. While it can be very disruptive, as the film crew will take over and rearrange your home entirely for a day or more, it pays well and you don't have to do any work. List your location at www.filmspace.co.za, www.tlcsa.co.za or www.cherry-picked.co.za.

This is only a selection of ideas for you to consider. I would also encourage you to register on recruitment websites with certain keywords relating to the areas that you are interested in. Also keep your eye on websites such as Gumtree, particularly under the 'Part-time & Weekend jobs' section.

Income generated from your side hustle will need to be declared on your tax return, and you may need to register as a provisional taxpayer. Remember, though, that expenses you incur in generating this income is tax deductible, so it's crucial that you keep proper records of your expenses. Speak to a tax consultant if you need advice.

Lastly, remember to always put a little of that extra money aside. Commit to a fixed amount, perhaps 10%, to put into a separate savings account. Side-hustle income is not guaranteed. It may develop into something permanent, but then again it may not, so nurture a small nest egg for the lean times, when you have little or no extra money coming in.

Chapter 12

Setting smart goals

'Be a doer, not a dreamer.'
– Shonda Rhimes

By now, you are well on your way to building wealth. By taking control of your money and changing your spending patterns, you are starting to think and act smarter when it comes to your money. We can now move on to the next steps in our journey to wealth:
- setting goals and other reasons to invest;
- learning about investing;
- discovering which type of investor you are; and
- choosing the investments that suit you best.

KNOW YOUR WHY

If you understand *why* you are doing something, your end goal will be clear. This will keep you motivated. Goals are not just about taking action, they're also about feelings and emotions, and these elements drive us to succeed. If you really *want* something on an emotional level, you will stay focused.

Life is always changing, and as we move through its different stages, we have various aspirations: things we want to achieve, places we want to visit, situations we want to experience. When we left school, we all imagined what our lives would look like in a few years' time. For many of us, the reality was quite different, and as we moved into the adult world, our ideas and goals changed. It's a continual process – as we move through life, we learn and grow as individuals, and our aspirations shift.

Sometimes we fail along the way. It's easy to become despondent, but there is nothing worse, to my mind, than giving up and living life from one day to the next, unsure of where you are going or what you hope to achieve.

Having a dream and a vision fuels our passion, gives us a reason to jump out of bed in the morning and provides direction in our lives. Some people are exceptionally driven by their dreams, which is highly admirable. I have one such friend, who doesn't see obstacles and doesn't allow himself to be deterred by issues along the way. Determined not to settle for less, he keeps moving forward.

DREAMS AND GOALS: THERE IS A DIFFERENCE

We all need dreams. It's part of the pleasure of life to be able to explore the vast corners of our minds and use our imagination in the most creative of ways. Often, our dreams are of the 'what if' or 'imagine if' nature, and their coming true depends largely on luck (as in the 'What if I won the lottery?' scenario). A dream has no specific plan, no agenda, no sense of priority.

Think about the dreams you had as a child. They were free and pure, untainted by the realities of life. They probably changed frequently, and there was never any clear plan for achieving them.

To make a dream a reality, we need to turn it into a goal and have a plan in place to achieve it. Goals are more tangible. It must be possible to visualise and experience them, and to know when you have achieved them. They are measurable. They are also rooted in reality, unlike dreams, which can be about almost anything.

Goals also need to be big to stretch us a little. Dreams stretch our imagination, but goals stretch our energy, our resourcefulness and our skills. By striving to achieve our goals, we learn and grow as individuals, which changes our lives forever. If we are not stretched or challenged, we can lead a stagnant life, just plodding along. As Michelangelo – painter, sculptor, architect and poet – once said: 'The greater danger for most of us lies not in setting our aim too high and falling short; but in setting our aim too low, and achieving our mark.'

SETTING SMART GOALS

Goals also have a cost, whereas dreams are free. To achieve our goals, we need to invest time, effort and money in them. It takes energy, and what we put in is what we'll get out. Because of that, they are valuable – it takes effort to achieve them, whereas dreams are passive and can change on a whim.

To achieve our goals, financial or otherwise, we need a plan. We need to be focused, and we need to take action. Dreams play an important role in motivating us, but dreams alone will not get us to where we want to be.

Many of our dreams have financial roots: we need money to make them happen. We may think that our goal is financial ('I want to be rich'), but money is just the enabler. We do not simply want money for the sake of having it, but rather to allow us to fulfil some desire. If you have a clear picture in your mind of what your goals are, and a plan to get there, you will definitely be more committed to achieving them than if they were merely a loose idea.

Why do you want money? Think about it. If you are not sure, try completing this sentence: 'If I had lots of money, I would …'

When people talk about having lots of money and getting rich as their goal in life, I am often reminded of the story of King Midas. Midas lived in ancient Greece with his daughter, Philomena, whom he adored. He was obsessed with money, however, and often spent days counting his gold coins.

One day, a stranger appeared at the gate. Midas invited him in, and saw that he was a friend of the god Dionysus. Midas allowed him to stay, and Dionysus so appreciated the kind gesture towards his friend that he granted the king one wish. King Midas wished for everything he touched to turn to gold so he would become the richest man in the world.

Dionysus kept his promise. King Midas was thrilled, and went around his palace using his new power, turning all kinds of things to gold. When he sat down to eat, though, he picked up a grape and it turned to gold. Soon, he became fearful. Then Philomena entered the room. Midas hugged her, turning her into a golden statue. Distressed, he begged Dionysus to remove the power, which he realised was more of a curse.

Dionysus did so, and Midas decided to share his vast fortune with his people. He became generous and grateful for everything in his life. Everybody loved him, and he was greatly mourned when he eventually passed away.

The moral of the story is, of course, that being driven by money is never a good thing. But it also shows how our perception of what is important can change, depending on our circumstances.

LIMITING THOUGHTS

It's good to dream. Some dreams may be little more than random thoughts, and others may distil themselves in our minds to become concrete goals that we want to achieve. We may get really fired up at the idea of them, and motivated to achieve them. We may even start visualising what things will look like once we have achieved them.

But then the limiting thoughts start creeping in. We may feel we've had a reality check. Some of these worries might be rational, but in many cases they are barriers we create in our own minds, preventing us from getting what we want out of life. These barriers may feel very real, but most often we can overcome them. All we need to do is consciously work at not letting them distract us.

Can you identify with any of these thoughts?

- **'I am not good enough.'** Maybe someone else is doing what you want to do, or someone you consider better than you is achieving what you want to achieve. Remember, everyone is different. Why would you want to copy others, anyway? Develop yourself, write your own story and look back with pride to see how far you have progressed.
- **'I have plenty of time.'** Procrastination is the silent dream-killer. If you put things off, you may never get there. Don't be fooled by time. It has a nasty way of marching on rapidly. Before you know it, it might be too late. Start today – set clear goals and develop a plan of action.
- **'What if I fail?'** How will you grow and learn unless you fail a few times along the way? Babies would never learn to walk if they had a fear of falling. Fear is a protective mechanism that keeps you safe and works hard to prevent you from being harmed, but it can work too

hard and conjure problems where there aren't any. Don't be afraid to fail, to fall down. You can get up again. It's all part of the growth process. Be prepared to fail, and be prepared, also, to grow as you learn.
- **'It's got to be perfect.'** Rome wasn't built in a day, and over-analysing could mean getting caught up in 'analysis paralysis'. You keep analysing and rehashing things to the extent that you never get started. Set goals and draw up a plan, but then get moving. You can adapt and change things as you go along, but it's critical to keep moving. Doing nothing eventually leads to stagnation, which is not going to get you anywhere.
- **'I have too much on my plate.'** With everything going on in our lives, it's easy to lose focus and fail to put energy and effort into achieving our goals, so don't set too many of them. Start, perhaps, with one simple goal. When you have achieved it, move on to another one. If achieving your goal is a high priority, arrange your actions around that goal and place it at the top of your list. Paying yourself first is a classic example: make investing in your dream or goal the first payment that you make at the end of the month.
- **'It's going to take too long.'** Impatience is something from which I suffer, so I identify with this one. We live in a society in which many things happen super-fast, so we expect everything to be like this. When we are striving towards a goal, however, too much too fast can be overwhelming. We are only human. We need time to absorb and process information and make the right decisions. Practise the art of patience and realise that all good things take time. When it comes to investing and making money, time is one of the most important factors.

Don't let these thoughts become barriers that hold you back – conquer them and move into action. Have a clear vision of where you want to be, set goals and develop your plan of action.

SETTING SMART GOALS

How do you go about setting goals for yourself, then? An acronym often used when speaking about goals is SMART. Smartwomen know that goals must be:

S – Specific
M – Measurable
A – Attainable
R – Relevant
T – Timeous

If all five of these elements are in place, your goal-setting process will be effective. If your goals are vague, you will have no idea where you are going. If they are not measurable, you won't be able to track your progress. If they are unrealistic and unattainable, you will get disappointed and lose interest. If they are not relevant, you will not be committed to them. And if they do not have a specific time frame, you won't be able to measure your progress.

Let's examine this in a finance example. Suppose your goal was to save up enough money to go on an extended cruise. You would look at the process as follows:

S – you are working towards a cruise
M – you know how much money you will need (the cost of the cruise)
A – based on your budget, you know how much you can set aside each month to reach your goal
R – it's on your bucket list, so it's very relevant!
T – it will take you two years to save up (you have worked this out)

If you try to achieve this goal in a shorter period, you may become disillusioned by the difficulty of saving more every month and then drop the goal altogether.

There are many areas in our lives in which we may want to set goals. Some may have financial ties. The team at www.mindtools.com gives some pointers:

- **Career:** What do you want to achieve, and by when? If you want to make a career change, to which career do you want to change, and by when?
- **Financial:** How much do you want to earn, and by when? Also, how does this relate to your career goals?

- **Education:** Do you want to enhance your qualifications, learn a foreign language, upskill yourself for a new job, etc.?
- **Family:** Do you want to have children?
- **Creative:** Do you have any artistic goals? Perhaps learn to play an instrument or write a book? What do you need to do to achieve these goals?
- **Attitude:** Do you feel a need to change part of your behaviour or mindset, because it is holding you back? Which steps do you need to take to achieve this?
- **Physical:** Do you need to make any changes to your health? What will you need to do to achieve this?

Write your goals down, list the steps you need to take to achieve them, and measure them regularly. Make sure you do not have too many goals at once, as you want to be able to focus effectively to achieve them. Remember, too, that some goals will be short-term (achievable within a year or two), and others may be long-term (they will take two to five years, or longer, to achieve).

It may be useful to break a big goal down into smaller goals to keep you motivated along the way. Perhaps you want to start your own business. You'll need to save up enough capital, but there are many smaller goals you need to achieve as well – researching your target market, the products and services you will offer, the price you will charge, the marketing or promotional activity that will work best, the skills you need to develop, and so on. All these can be smaller goals on their own, with specific timelines.

You could also break a big financial goal down into smaller components. Let's say you need R200 000 to start the business, and set the goal of saving R50 000 in a year's time, then another R50 000 in another year, and so on. Measure your progress so that you can see how well you are doing, and stay on track. Reward yourself as you reach your goals, and celebrate your success. It is always motivating and rewarding to look back and see how far you have come.

VISION BOARDS

Another useful tool that many people use is vision boards. As its name indicates, it's a visual manifestation of a goal. Instead of writing your goal down on paper, you set it up on a board, using images or words, and display it in a prominent place where you can see it all the time. It can help you clarify what you want to achieve in life and keep you focused, as it's a constant reminder of what you are striving to achieve.

One of the reasons for doing this is that the mind responds very well to visual stimuli. Seeing your goals will strengthen your connection to them and your motivation to achieve them. Find pictures and words that represent your goals and place them on the board. You may even want to include a picture of yourself. Choose words and pictures that inspire and motivate you. Don't overcrowd the board – leave space on the board, and in your life, for you to be able to achieve your goals. Chaos achieves little, so keep it neat.

You can include more than one goal on your vision board, but you might want to develop individual boards for various purposes. Perhaps your financial and career goals will be on a separate board to your personal goals. See what works for you.

Place your vision boards somewhere where you can see them regularly – this constant visual reminder will help to keep you focused. It may also be useful to note the date on which you created it, so that you can use this as a means of measurement when you achieve your goals. A picture is worth a thousand words, the saying goes, which is exactly what a vision board is all about.

* * *

As you work on building wealth and getting rich, make sure there is a clear goal behind it. It can be daunting to try to achieve your financial goals on your own. Some people manage it alone, but others need the discipline and help of an objective professional to craft an effective plan and to help them stay on track, as there will always be distractions. You may start out with good intentions, but life happens and shifts your focus elsewhere. To counter this, you could enlist the help of a professional financial adviser who will draw up a tailor-made plan that starts with your goals and ends with a clear, simple road map to follow.

If you are confident enough to do it alone, then by all means set your own financial goals and draw up a plan for achieving them. There is a plethora of information available about investing, and many factors to be taken into account (more about this later, in Chapters 17 to 22), but by following the simple steps here, and putting a realistic plan in place, you will achieve your goals and see your dreams come true!

List your life goals and see how many of them have financial implications. Use this goal-setting sheet as the basis for your financial planning.

Goal-setting sheet

Goal description	Why is it important to you?	What do you need to do to achieve it?	How will you measure it?	Time frame	Impacts on other areas of your life/ other goals

Chapter 13

Retire rich

'If you're given a choice between money and sex appeal, take the money. As you get older, the money will become your sex appeal.'

– Katharine Hepburn

Many of us dream of not having to go to work in the mornings, of having the luxury of doing whatever we feel like with our time. This is retirement by another name, a point we can reach at 40, 50 or whatever age we choose. It's not about the age at which you will stop working, but about having enough money to be able to do so.

How do we get there and is there a shortcut? It appears there is indeed, for some people! I recently learnt something about an elderly woman I have known for quite a few years. I first met her when she and her husband lived in an affluent suburb in a beautiful home, where they'd raised a family and lived a good life. Her husband passed away, and she sold the house a while later. She then used some of the proceeds to buy a unit in a luxurious retirement complex and had plenty of cash left to invest to provide herself with a comfortable income.

When I met her again, she filled me in on the finer details of her story. She'd grown up in a fabulous home that belonged to her parents, and when they passed, she inherited it. This was the house she'd shared with her husband and children. This struck me as a wonderful story of intergenerational wealth. If only life were that easy for everyone! For most of us, myself included, the road to wealth and financial freedom is a bit more challenging.

Accumulating enough money to retire on takes time, and the earlier we start, the easier it is. The irony is that when we are young, we have many pressing financial issues to worry about and typically put retirement savings on the back burner. We are busy building our careers, and we may be looking to get married and start a family. Retirement planning is an interesting discussion point I have with younger clients. It's difficult for them to imagine turning 50 or 60, never mind having to save for that time in their lives. Yet I know that if they stick with my advice and start investing at an early age, they will be truly grateful by the time they reach middle age.

Planning for retirement is not generally a hot topic at the dinner table either. You may hear people talk about the share tip that's going to triple in value, or the property deal that is too good to pass over, but seldom is the conversation about the fantastic investment plan that will give them financial freedom later in life.

The luxury of having enough money in old age is the ultimate definition of 'rich'. The secret is to build up enough assets over time to support your lifestyle without you having to work by exchanging time for money. You can generate an income from different sources: rental property, dividends from shares, income from retirement annuities or a pension fund, for example.

For now, we will consider the traditional ways in which people accumulate wealth for retirement – through employer-provided benefits or private retirement funding through retirement annuities – as these are the most common forms of accumulating wealth for retirement. We'll discuss other ways of accumulating wealth later on, when we examine various investment options.

THE WORLD OF WORK HAS CHANGED

The world of work today is very different from how it was in our parents' and grandparents' time. Many people in previous generations worked for one employer for most of their lives, and retired around age 60 or 65. They probably belonged to a company pension fund and were given a guaranteed pension based on their years of service. They received annual increases and life after retirement was fairly affordable, as the pension fund took care of their expenses. When they passed away, in all likelihood there was an inheritance for the children.

The challenge for those who didn't belong to a pension fund was to build up enough assets to sustain them in old age. Smart people managed to do so and, if you didn't live too long after retirement, or if you continued to invest well, it was entirely possible to survive off your pension payout. But not everyone was as lucky. I recall a man who retired in his sixties with a substantial share portfolio and a property in an affluent suburb. He and his wife were considered well off and continued to live comfortably, but unfortunately the ravages of inflation had eroded his investments over the years. By their eighties they were almost destitute, and had to sell their home and move in with their daughter.

So, retirement savings can all work out reasonably well if you retire at 60 or 65 and your life expectancy is 10 or 15 years; you should have enough money to survive. The problem today (as with my friend's parents) is that life expectancy is increasing. Most people cannot save enough money or build up enough assets to sustain them until death. It's a sad day when the money runs out and we have to turn to our children, the state or someone else, to assist us. Many people today are caring for parents who have simply outlived their money.

LIVING LONGER, BATTLING MORE

The longer you live, the longer your money has to last – and in this fact lies the heart of the problem. According to the Royal Geographical Society, during the time of the Roman Empire, life expectancy was about 22 to 25. In 1900, world life expectancy was approximately 30. By 1985, it was about 62.

In South Africa today, 60-year-olds can expect to live another 16.5 years on average, according to data analysed by Knoema IT Solutions. These are averages, of course, and many people live well into their eighties and nineties. The main problem is that no one knows when exactly they will die, so ensuring that you have enough money to be comfortable, right up to your last breath, is pretty much a hit-and-miss game.

However, we need to try our best to make sure that we have more than we need. The idea is that our money must outlive us, and not the other way around. We can only accumulate assets while earning money – wealth can't be created out of nothing – so we need to be smart about work and make sure we build up assets to sustain us beyond 80. The other thing to remember is that while many people will remain economically active beyond age 60 or 65, it not a given that they will be able to make enough money to live. A healthy nest egg allows people choices. Wouldn't it be wonderful to have money to travel and enjoy life without the pressure of having to earn a living?

So, what are the best ways to save for retirement? There are many options, and a combination of vehicles often delivers the best results. Remember, too, that there are distinct tax advantages for approved retirement-funding investment vehicles. The government is trying to encourage retirement savings, and its retirement reform initiatives have been slowly implemented over the past few years.

EMPLOYER RETIREMENT FUNDS: PENSION AND PROVIDENT FUNDS

Let's start with the pension or provident fund. Employers are under no legal obligation to provide their staff with retirement benefits, but many businesses do this voluntarily. Both the employer and employee usually contribute, so it's an extra benefit for the employee – an addition to the salary you are paid. The concept of 'cost to company' refers to the total amount that your employer is paying you in cash, plus other benefits such as a pension or provident fund contribution, or a medical aid contribution.

When you start your first job, seeing that pension fund deduction on your payslip each month may irk you a little. In reality, it's the best thing ever for your long-term wealth. Starting early – in your twenties – is a sure-fire recipe for having an abundance of money in your fifties or sixties. For many people, the pension or provident fund is the greatest amount of money they manage to accumulate in their entire lives. It is their greatest asset.

Pension funds vs. provident funds

What is the major difference between a pension fund and provident fund? Historically, the most important difference was how the funds could be accessed at retirement, but this changed with legislation that came into effect in 2021. Prior to 1 March 2021, 100% of the proceeds from a provident fund could be taken in cash at retirement, whereas with a pension fund, only one-third could be taken in cash at retirement, and the rest had to be used to purchase an annuity (pension). From 1 March 2021, the rules around provident funds changed to bring them more in line with pension funds. For existing provident and provident preservation fund members over the age of 55, 100% of benefits can still be taken in cash at retirement (they are unaffected by the new legislation). For provident and provident preservation fund members under 55, all benefits and growth as at 1 March 2021 can still be taken at 100% cash at retirement, but all new contributions and growth from 1 March 2021 can only be taken as one-third in cash, and the balance used to purchase an annuity.

There is one further complication when it comes to pension funds: there are two types. These are defined benefit funds and defined contribution funds. Traditionally, all pension funds used to be defined benefit funds – the fund rules specify how benefits will be calculated at retirement, based on years of service.

Here's an example. The fund rules could state that a member will receive 2% of their final salary for every year for which they contributed to the pension fund. So, after 20 years, the pension will be about 40% of the member's final salary, after 30 years 60%, and so on. To receive approximately the same pension as the salary that an employee was earning at retirement, the member would need to contribute to that pension fund for about 50 years! Of course, this is not possible, so even with this system there were retirement shortfalls.

When you consider that a 75% replacement ratio is a rough industry standard (which means that your post-retirement income should equate to 75% of your final salary), then working for a company with a defined benefit fund for 35 years or so could give you a pretty comfortable retirement. This was largely the story of past generations.

Final salary here refers to net salary – that is, before deductions – but can exclude additional benefits such as a housing or travel allowance. This is merely an illustration, and all pension funds have their own rules that stipulate how benefits are paid, and on what basis these are calculated. If you are a member of a pension fund, it is advisable to familiarise yourself with your pension fund rules and understand how they will affect your planning and financial goals. Speak to your HR department or enlist the help of a professional financial adviser if you need help figuring it all out.

Today, the Government Employees Pension Fund is the largest pension fund in Africa. It is still a defined benefit fund, and in 2021 it had over 1.2 million active members and over 450 000 pensioners and beneficiaries.

In the early 1990s, South Africans started moving from defined benefit pension funds to defined contribution pension funds. Instead of having a guaranteed pension based on a fixed formula, the member would decide how they wanted to invest the pension fund benefits to provide themselves with an income (pension).

Understanding the tax implications

Both the employee's and the employer's contributions towards a pension or provident fund are tax deductible (up to certain limits) for the employee. So, the amount that you and your employer contribute towards your pension or provident fund is deducted from your income before your tax is calculated. The employer's contribution is added back to the employee's salary as a fringe benefit and is taxed accordingly. In effect, this means that you get a tax deduction for your contribution, as the deduction for your employer's contribution is offset by the fringe benefit that is added to your salary. Your contribution reduces your taxable income, so you pay less tax.

Once you retire, you pay tax on the lump sum as well as the monthly pension that you receive. A portion of the lump sum is taxed at 0% and the balance is taxed at preferential rates.

A company pension or provident fund is an excellent benefit. Aside from the obvious fact that you are benefitting from your employer contributing to your retirement, these funds often also have other benefits, called risk benefits. These provide money in case of death, disability, and so on. If it is compulsory for you to join the pension or provident fund, be happy that you are being forced to save. If it is optional, be smart and join as soon as you can.

Some companies prefer to pay their employees an additional amount in cash instead of having a company pension or provident fund. The argument is that employees must make their own retirement provision, with the employer giving them extra money to do so. In reality, very few employees invest that money – it simply gets sucked into the household budget and spent. Being forced to save is paying yourself first, by default!

DON'T CASH IN

Very few people work for the same employer for their entire career. However, your retirement fund is linked to your employer. So, when you leave the company, you can either take your proceeds in cash, or you can have them paid into a preservation fund, which will carry on growing until you reach retirement age.

It is always tempting to take the cash, but it's the worst possible idea. Once that money is spent, it's almost impossible to make it up again in future. If you join a new retirement fund, you may be able to 'buy back' years, but this will take money out of your monthly budget over and above your current contributions, and you may still not be able to make up for all the investment growth you have lost.

The smart thing to do is to preserve your retirement benefits and to continue investing for retirement. Cash paid out to you at resignation or retrenchment is not a windfall; it is money intended for your retirement and represents a time in your life you cannot reclaim. You will also pay tax on any money you withdraw from your retirement fund. At the time of writing, the first R25 000 is not taxed, with the balance taxed according to a specific tax table. This tax is an unnecessary expense, and money that you cannot make up easily again.

Even if you preserve all your benefits and contribute your entire working career, longevity means that there will invariably be shortfalls. So, it is a good idea to supplement your benefits with additional investments, such as a retirement annuity.

The 'portable pension fund': retirement annuities
A retirement annuity (RA) is a long-term savings plan specifically designed to allow you to save for retirement. The contributions are tax deductible up to certain limits and you cannot access the money until you are at least 55. It's called a 'portable pension fund' because *you* own it, and not your employer, so it is not affected when you change jobs, as it simply moves with you.

At retirement, you can withdraw up to one-third of the total value of your RA as a lump sum, while the balance is paid in the form of a regular income (pension). One of the great advantages of an RA is that creditors cannot seize it in the event of insolvency, so it is a safe way of investing if you have your own business. The money is also locked in: you cannot access it before retirement at age 55, which removes any temptation to spend it beforehand. You cannot surrender it or take out a loan against it; if you stop paying premiums, it simply remains intact until you reach retirement age or age 55, whichever you prefer.

Premiums are also tax deductible, alongside pension and provident fund contributions, up to certain limits. So, there is an added bonus to saving with an RA, which we discuss in more detail in Chapter 22.

OLD IS NOT OLD ANY MORE
The face of retirement has changed compared to previous generations. People are healthier; many are still working into their sixties and even their seventies. Having money at retirement gives you choices: you could start a small business, travel or simply do charity work. You don't want to work because you have to, although it may be a reality if you left your planning too late. Without money in the form of a solid retirement nest egg, the thought of reaching retirement age can be terrifying.

Accumulating that nest egg takes time and requires good investment decisions. You may be unsure where to start, or you may have started saving but are not sure whether you are saving enough. The smart move is to get advice. The process is not an exact science and is based on assumptions about interest rates and inflation, but, in essence, there are three variables on which retirement planning rests:

- the age at which you want to retire;
- the amount of money you want as an income; and
- how long you expect to live.

The first two are easy to answer. The third less so, but we can make assumptions about life expectancy. As I've said, it's not an exact science, but getting advice and crunching the numbers is way better than doing nothing and hoping for that inheritance or lottery win. Speaking of inheritance: your parents are probably going to eat up all your inheritance and knock on your door for you to support them!

Consider which types of investment you are comfortable with and know enough about. You don't want to make mistakes – there is no second chance.

I'm often asked when one should start investing for retirement. The answer is simple – when you receive your first salary. If you are past that point, start tomorrow. It's better than next month, or next year.

DELAY STARTING AND PAY THE PRICE

It's often difficult for someone under 30 to imagine why they need to start investing as early as possible. The reason is that the longer you leave it, the more difficult it is to achieve the same result.

Let's say you wanted to accumulate R10 million by the age of 60. For simplicity's sake, we will ignore inflation. The following table gives an indication of how much you would need to invest every month, assuming that your monthly contribution does not increase and your money grows by either 10 or 12% per annum, on average.

The benefit of early investment

Start investing at age	Number of years to invest to reach age 60	Monthly amount you need to invest (10% average growth per annum)	Monthly amount you need to invest (12% average growth per annum)
25	35	R2 942	R1 831
30	30	R4 847	R3 276
35	25	R8 108	R5 930
40	20	R13 922	R10 974
45	15	R25 097	R21 210
50	10	R50 034	R45 059

R10 million may sound like an enormous amount of money, but it won't be enough for someone aged 30 today. We haven't even considered the impact of inflation over time, but the cost of delaying is clear from the figures in the table. The higher the growth rate, the less you need to invest, but you cannot escape the fact that, if you have time on your side, you would be a fool not to use it.

Apart from the cost of delaying, waiting until later in life could have other implications. I read an article in the newspaper a while ago in which a spokesperson for a financial services company said that it's fine for people not to start saving in their twenties. They can start in their thirties, and would just have to save a bit more every month.

This is true, but the spokesperson completely overlooked one important aspect: people generally get married around the age of 30 and have children a few years later. Once you start a family, expenses rocket. There is no spare money for anything. So, instead of being able to invest more, the average person will probably have less money to invest – another excellent reason for starting early. Start before family responsibilities take priority!

Of course, the other advantage of starting early is that you get used to not having that money in your hands to spend. If you get into the habit of putting money aside from the outset, you will never have it in your monthly budget to spend. Again, it's a case of paying yourself before you pay anyone else.

It's often difficult to get this message through to younger people – retirement is just too far away. Perhaps the word 'retirement' itself is the problem. It sounds like old people! Think of it, instead, as financial freedom or getting rich. It all refers to the same thing – the point at which you have enough money to stop formal employment (if you wish), leaving you with the precious luxury of deciding how to spend your time.

Can you accumulate enough assets to have money until your last breath? This is debatable. I'm sometimes shocked at the figures the calculators churn out. It is often useful to learn from the wisdom of others. The Sanlam Benchmark Survey conducts research among retirees who receive a pension either from a pension fund or an RA. In the 2016 survey, only 35% believed they had saved up enough for the rest of their lives, and a staggering 48% said that their income was not enough to cover their daily living expenses. It is also interesting to note that 23% said they still had children who were dependent on them!

The overwhelming response, when respondents were asked what advice they would give to younger people, was to start saving earlier and to learn about different investment options.

Being smart means that your retirement provision will not only take the form of savings in a pension fund or RA. There are other ways of accumulating capital – through property, shares and a host of other investment options, which we discuss later. When you stop formal employment, you can keep investing and growing your wealth.

The world of work and retirement has changed dramatically. Today, many people are self-employed, take early retirement, or face retrenchment or other issues that prevent them from working until 'normal' retirement. People are reinventing themselves, starting new businesses, and working into their seventies and beyond.

Retirement is not an end. It is the start of a new and exciting stage of your life. The important thing, though, is to have choices – and money gives us these choices. Here are some tips for retiring rich:
- Retire debt-free.
- Start saving as soon as possible. Even if you have a pension or provident fund, you will need additional savings.

- Do not cash in your pension or provident fund benefits if you change jobs.
- Use windfalls, such as your annual bonus, to boost your retirement savings.
- Get advice on how much you will need and how you can get there. Don't leave your retirement planning to chance.
- If you do not have enough money to retire, upskill yourself and keep working.

Chapter 14

Fast money, burnt fingers

> 'The four most dangerous words in investing are "this time it's different".'
>
> – *Sir John Templeton*

We all want to make money, and we want to make it now! Some people may find that they haven't saved up enough and need to play catch-up. Others may be taken in by the allure of getting rich fast. Still others may see investing as an easy way to get out of the poverty cycle. For whichever reason, thousands of people have fallen for investment opportunities that promise the earth but deliver dust. There may be widespread media coverage when these schemes go under and everyone looks on in horror, but then the next clever idea comes along, and people start investing all over again.

The reality, of course, is that there is no easy way to make money – not legally, anyway. Get-rich-quick schemes, such as Ponzi or pyramid schemes, have cost many people their hard-earned money and even their lives. There are many examples of these schemes, and new ones keep popping up. They initially seem to offer wonderful investment returns, but once they start folding there is little hope of recovering any money that has been invested. Many investors in Ponzi schemes put in the little bit of money they have, and losing it has a devastating impact on their lives.

A tragic example of this was Aneesa Arrison, a 43-year-old Cape Town mother of four who shot her children and herself in January 2017 after losing an investment of R1 million – her late husband's pension money – in a suspected Ponzi scheme called 4th Power Investments. Only one of her sons, aged 14, survived. The scheme had stopped paying investors in September 2016, and the director of 4th Power Investments, Pastor David Cupido of Touws River in the Western Cape, was investigated by the Hawks on charges of fraud, theft, money laundering and contravening sections of the Financial Advisory and Intermediary Services (FAIS) Act and the Banks Act.

In another example of 'black collar' crime, Colin Davids, a pastor at the New Direction Church in Parow, Cape Town, and director of the Platinum Forex Group (PFG), had apparently taken deposits of about R330 million from around 2 000 investors, offering unrealistic returns of up to 84%, until he was arrested in 2016 for contravening the Banks Act and the FAIS Act. His lavish lifestyle included owning two multi-million-rand homes in Plattekloof and Hermanus, as well as two BMWs and a Jaguar F-Type V8 S convertible. It was estimated that only around R100 million remained of all the money he had received from investors, and this had to be shared between them.

Ponzi schemes are often hard to spot because of the charismatic personalities that design and promote them and the clever marketing they use. But let's take a step back and understand exactly what these schemes are, and why they are doomed to fail.

WHAT IS A PONZI SCHEME?

In short, a Ponzi scheme is a fraudulent investment structure that is not backed by any kind of legitimate business. The grandpa of this concept was Italian-born Charles Ponzi, who perfected a scheme using coupons for priority airmail stamps. Operating from Boston in the United States, he attracted investors with promises of abnormally high returns. Under intense media scrutiny, the scheme eventually folded in 1920. Ponzi was sentenced to 14 years in prison for mail fraud, and died penniless in Rio de Janeiro in 1949.

Nearly one hundred years later, Ponzi schemes are still coming at us thick and fast. They may look like very different types of businesses or investments, but they all work in basically the same way: they lure potential investors with promises of extraordinarily high returns for little effort. In another version of this scam, known as a pyramid scheme, though, victims are put under great pressure to recruit new investors in order to make returns. Operators of such schemes use the money from the many new investors to pay handsome returns to a small group of earlier investors who brought in recruits (i.e., it's a pyramid structure). The scheme is doomed to collapse as the number of members grows, however: not enough money can flow in to sustain the promised payouts to investors.

Some very creative Ponzi schemes have captured our imagination over the years. Here are a few.

The biggest scam in American history

In 2009, Bernard 'Bernie' Madoff was sentenced to 150 years in prison for running the biggest Ponzi scheme in American history. As a well-respected financier, he managed to con thousands of investors out of $65 billion over decades. Things fell apart in 2008, when Madoff found himself struggling to meet his clients' payout requests, which totalled about $7 billion. In the past he had simply paid them from the existing pool of funds in his bank account, but by the end of that year he only had between $200 and $300 million left. Very few investors recouped their losses, and Madoff died in prison in April 2021.

The rotten-milk beauty range

One of the biggest scams in South African history was the Kubus scheme in the 1980s. Adriaan Nieuwoudt convinced investors to buy a milk culture for use in beauty products. For R500, investors received a dried product they would add to a glass of milk. This milk would then produce ten jars of culture per week, which was dried and sold back to Nieuwoudt. He paid R10 per envelope or R100 per week, allowing investors to break even within five weeks. The dried products were ground up and resold to new investors; no beauty product was ever manufactured. The scheme was exported to the United States in 1984, and eventually declared an illegal lottery by the South African government, which shut it down. By that stage, investors had put R140 million of their money into the scheme.

The miracle that wasn't
In another incredible story, Sibusiso Radebe's Miracle 2000 scheme promised investors a return of 200% after 42 days. All they had to pay was a registration fee of R50 and a minimum investment of R300. In January 2000, investors queued in the street outside Radebe's house to sign up. In mid-July, the police raided his home and arrested him on charges of theft, fraud and breaking banking laws. It is reported that he had been raking in an unbelievable R3 million per day! Many customers were enraged that he'd been arrested and arrived in court to support him, claiming that Radebe was running a black empowerment scheme aimed at helping impoverished people change their lives. He eventually pleaded guilty and admitted to having accepted investments amounting to over R36 million from at least 13 324 people.

Fidentia
In 2007, the Fidentia scandal broke, leading to the arrest and conviction of its mastermind, J. Arthur Brown, who had used the savings of 47 000 widows and orphans to fund a lavish lifestyle. Investors had been lured with high investment returns, but there was little to back this. In total, Brown squandered an estimated R500 million. In 2014, he was sentenced to 15 years in prison for fraud, but released on parole in October 2021, after having served only seven years.

The Wealth Hub
The Wealth Hub, an online stokvel, was declared illegal and had its bank accounts frozen after attracting over 20 000 investors. It cost R295 per month to become a member, ostensibly to cover initial costs for travel, and for financial and personal-development training material. Once you completed the training, you paid R100 to join the stokvel. In typical pyramid fashion, each member of the scheme was required to recruit 39 new members for a fee of R200 each. By the time you had recruited the

required 39 members, you would have made R7 800 and would graduate to the next level. Once investors reached the third level, they would collect R156 000 from new members. Each time investors graduated to a higher level, they were charged an increasing administration fee, payable directly to The Wealth Hub. It was closed down in 2015.

MMM

The MMM Ponzi scheme keeps reinventing itself. It started in Russia in 1989, was closed down in the 1990s, and reopened in 2011 as MMM Global in numerous countries, including South Africa. MMM SA members were promised between 30 and 40% in returns for paying other people money on request. This donation model has been described as a pyramid scheme by most financial experts, although there is heated debate about whether MMM is a Ponzi scheme. In 2016, the Hawks launched an investigation into MMM. MMM is not regulated by the Financial Sector Conduct Authority (FSCA) or the South African Reserve Bank, so investors have no recourse. The South African arm collapsed in May 2016 and reopened for investors in 2017, using cyber-currency linked to Bitcoin – which is very difficult to trace.

YOU CAN'T MAKE MONEY OUT OF THIN AIR

None of the schemes described here had or have any business activities that can generate the profits they need to pay investors. Their business is simply to rake money in.

I attended an investment presentation some years back. I had been invited by a friend, who had heard from another friend that this was a great way to invest, with good returns. I sat in the audience, wondering what this business was about – there was no mention of a product being manufactured. It was a holiday-club type of investment, but the details about the actual holiday units were hazy. Needless to say, I left politely and kept my purse firmly closed!

There are some ingenious people behind these schemes. They design cleverly worded marketing campaigns and make alluring promises that appeal to our desire to make money quickly and easily. You may also

encounter some very charismatic individuals who claim to have made millions by investing in this way, and who now want to share their secret with you. It's easy to get caught up in the hype, but be smart. Stay on the lookout for these serious red flags:
- promises of abnormally high returns in a short period of time;
- 'secret formulas' or business concepts that can only be shared with selected investors;
- guaranteed returns;
- vague business models – if you don't understand it, don't invest;
- promises that the more people you recruit, the more money you will make; and
- pressure to reinvest your earnings.

Understand what is real and possible when investing. When you look at investment returns, find out what is realistic by comparing it with what banks and other financial service companies are offering. Be wary of investments that offer returns way in excess of this. All this hinges on knowledge: if you know the basics, you won't be taken in so easily. Ignorance plays a major role in getting caught up in these schemes.

Follow the old adage that, if it seems too good to be true, it *is* too good to be true. Don't be comforted if the scheme has paid out to family members or other investors. It's possible that they are also being scammed and just don't know it yet.

The Financial Sector Conduct Authority (FSCA) oversees the non-banking financial services industry in South Africa. All businesses dealing with investments and money (that are not banks) must be registered with the FSCA. Before you consider investing anywhere, ask whether the scheme is registered with the FSCA, and request proof. Even this approach may not always be foolproof, so check directly with the FSCA (visit www.fsca.co.za, or call 080 020 3722). If a scheme is not registered with the FSCA, stay far away.

Chapter 15

How much are you worth?

'Money looks better in the bank than on your feet.'

– Sophia Amoruso

How do you measure your wealth? And what is wealth anyway? It's not how much money you have in the bank – that's just your cash flow. You manage cash flow with your budget, which has to do with money coming in and flowing out, and it changes almost daily.

Wealth is a bit more complex. It's a measurement of your accumulated assets (the sum of what you have built up so far) less what you owe. We measure our wealth by our net worth:

Net worth = Assets – Liabilities

Net worth is also an indication of financial health, as it reflects everything we have earned and spent up to a particular point in time. You can work out your net worth using the worksheet on page 134, but first, let's unpack and understand the concept of net worth.

If your liabilities exceed your assets (i.e., you owe more than you own) your net worth is negative. This is obviously not healthy or desirable. It is important to realise that net worth usually increases over time. Young people who are starting out generally have a lower net worth (perhaps even a negative one) than people who have been working for longer; their salaries are low, they may have student debt and they may incur other debt to start acquiring assets. As they progress in their careers, they start earning more, their assets increase and they reduce large debts such as home loans. They will also invest more when they can afford to, further growing their net worth.

Net worth can be affected by factors beyond your control, such as the value of an investment dropping due to market forces (a dip in the property or equity market), or unexpected events such as retrenchment or the loss of a business, forcing you to liquidate some assets. You may acquire a new asset but incur more debt to purchase it (such as when buying a more expensive home, or even a holiday home).

So, net worth is not a stagnant number. It fluctuates all the time, but it should show a steady increase over the years if you are making the right decisions and making financial progress.

Once you reach retirement, you may find that your net worth starts to decrease because you need to live off the assets you have accumulated. But if you invest smartly after retirement, your net worth can continue to grow.

So, the more we increase our net worth, the 'wealthier' we become. We can be fooled into thinking that we are increasing our net worth by increasing our assets, but if we are using debt to do this, we run the risk of decreasing our net worth if the asset does not perform as expected. As a general rule, never go into debt to fund an investment, as there are too many variables affecting this decision. One exception to this may be investing in a rental property, as this generates an income, so you will receive immediate benefit from the investment and have someone else pay the debt while the asset grows in value.

Calculating your net worth is a relatively simple exercise, but before you start, you need to understand what is classified as an asset and what is classified as a liability.

ASSETS AND LIABILITIES

The traditional definition of assets is that they are things that we own and that can be converted into cash at any point. Liabilities are things we owe to people, notably our debts. A new train of thought in recent years defines an asset as something that generates an income. If it doesn't, it's a liability, because it costs us money. This includes our primary residence, which is counter-intuitive to everything that we have been brought up to believe.

DEFINING ASSETS

I find this alternative definition of an asset simplistic. It is sensationalist and certainly sparks debate, but it can mean very little in the average person's quest to grow their wealth.

First, it ignores the complexity of our lives. We are not driven purely by building wealth. We build wealth while living our lives, and we need a home as well as material items (such as a boat or caravan) that add value, provide stability and enrich our lives. Many of these can later be sold and converted into cash. They may not generate an income, and may cost money to insure, but they are definitely assets – as is your home. They are just not *investment* assets. Rather, they may be classified as lifestyle assets – they won't make you rich in material terms, but will certainly enhance your quality of life.

Second, what about our other possessions? What about cash in the bank? It costs money to keep it there (in bank charges), so is it a liability? What about Krugerrands? You bought them as an investment, but you need to pay to insure and, perhaps, store them safely, so are they also a liability?

Putting everything into separate boxes based on whether something makes money or costs money is an oversimplified view that can skew your financial decisions. We need to consider a deeper dimension: we spend money on things either as part of our lifestyle (a personal-use asset) or for investment purposes (an investment asset). Our motives for buying them differ, as does the value they offer us. If we understand this, we can make sound financial decisions that will grow our long-term wealth. Everything we own ultimately forms part of our assets and net worth.

We derive different benefits from our assets as well – either a current benefit (we enjoy these assets as part of our lifestyle, or they generate some kind of income) or a future benefit (these assets grow in value and we can sell them at a profit at some point). It is important to realise that not all assets deliver the same return, and this diversity contributes to our overall wealth.

The obvious risk we run, if we assume that our primary residence is a significant part of our investments, is that we can spend too much money on this asset when we should be investing elsewhere to build wealth. Too much money spent on a primary residence means less money to invest elsewhere.

It takes time to make money, to build our net worth and our wealth. But this doesn't happen in isolation. Our money, our lifestyle, our spending and our investing are all intertwined, and we build wealth in the context and the richness of our lives. It is all about quality of life today, and financial security and wealth tomorrow – that balance we spoke about earlier.

We need to satisfy our basic human needs – a roof over our heads, safe transport, proper nutrition and healthy human interaction. Owning our own home, car and other items – such as a boat, or even personal effects – is linked to our sense of security and enjoyment. These items have less to do with investing and more to do with quality of life. Investing in our quality of life and investing to make a profit later are two separate agendas. However, in both cases we invest in items that can be liquidated (turned into cash). These are called assets.

So, in the debate about whether your primary residence is an asset, I believe that the definition of an asset as something that generates income is flawed. The question should rather be whether your primary residence is a good investment (or an investment at all) – an entirely different discussion, which I will deal with in Chapter 16.

LIABILITIES AND CASH FLOW

The term 'liabilities' refers to money we owe. Just as all assets are not equal, however, so all liabilities are not equal. Credit card debt, personal loans, and so on, are not the same as a home loan on a rental property. If you used the bank's money to purchase a property from which you receive rental income, you may have a 'liability' that does not affect your cash flow negatively, as some other liabilities do.

Your budget gives you an indication of your cash flow – what is coming in and what is going out. It is entirely possible to have a very healthy net worth, but also a cash flow problem – if your assets are tied up and not generating an income, or if you have high debt that you need to service monthly. Increasing your income or decreasing your debt are the only two levers you can pull to improve cash flow.

Cash flow is a very short-term view of your wealth. Net worth sums up your overall financial position from a longer-term perspective. By measuring your net worth on a regular basis, you can track your progress in building wealth over time.

Use the worksheet that follows to list your assets and liabilities and get an idea of your net worth. Review it annually to track your progress.

YOUR NET WORTH WORKSHEET

List your assets and liabilities. The difference between these is your net worth.

Assets			Liabilities
Shares, unit trusts		Credit card debt	
Pension or provident fund		Overdraft or personal loans	
Cash		Store card credit	
Policies		Home loan debt – primary residence	
Retirement annuities		Home loan debt – rental property	
Property – primary residence		Business loans	
Property – investment or holiday home		Car loan	
Boat, caravan, etc			
Car (1)			
Car (2)			
Jewellery and personal effects			
Art, collectibles			
Total assets		**Total liabilities**	
Total assets			
Less total liabilities			
Net worth			

Chapter 16

Is your home your nest egg?

'The ache for home lives in all of us. The safe place where we can go as we are and not be questioned.'

– Maya Angelou

Most of us were brought up to believe that owning our own home is a cornerstone of financial well-being, and one of our greatest assets. Your home is an asset, but whether it's your greatest one is debatable. Personally, I believe that the average person's retirement savings could be their greatest asset – it's often the largest amount of money an individual will ever amass in their lifetime.

We use the word 'investment' loosely when speaking about our homes, and many people consider their home to be a critical part of their overall wealth. But is it really? And is it smart to consider it an investment?

The Old Mutual Savings and Investment Monitor is an annual survey that measures South Africans' savings and investment behaviours and attitudes. According to their research in 2019, around 30% of people are relying on their home to provide a nest egg for old age. It is unclear whether this is because people have simply failed to plan properly for retirement, or whether they genuinely consider their primary residence to be a good investment. Either way, it's not the wisest of plans: after retirement, you need a roof over your head as well as money to live off; seldom can one property meet both needs.

How much of an investment is your home, though? The South African house price index, as supplied by Rode & Associates, provides perspective.

At the time of writing, over the very long term (20 years), property prices in South Africa had risen by 3.4% above inflation on average. Over the shorter term, the picture is less rosy, owing to a weakening economy: over the past 10 and 15 years, house prices have decreased in value by 0.3% compared to inflation. It is important to bear in mind that I am only considering capital appreciation here (increase in value of the property), and not the income that would be generated in the case of an investment property. This is discussed in more detail in Chapter 21.

There are many other investments that can deliver a far better return than growth on property, but we must also remember that the house price index figures quoted are averages across South Africa. There are many exceptions: property is all about timing and there are people who have managed to buy a property at a really good price and then sell it for an excellent profit. Location plays a crucial role, and the Cape Town metropole has exceeded the growth rates of other areas, achieving inflation-beating growth in the past 10, 15 and 20 years, as these regional property prices benefitted from semigration (moving from one part of a country to another) and perceived better governance.

When purchasing a property, there are many other costs to consider: rates, maintenance, interest on your home loan, etc. The overall property inflation figures do not take this into account; these numbers are based on house prices only. The interest alone can be a killer. For example, if you take out a loan of R1.5 million over 20 years at an interest rate of 7%, you will pay back R2 791 076 in total.

Your monthly repayment on that bond would be R11 629. But, paying off a bit extra every month could save you thousands in interest. An extra R1 000 a month (bringing the repayment to R12 629 per month) would save you R227 940 in interest and reduce the term of your loan to just under 17 years. The smart thing to do is to pay off your home loan in the shortest possible time.

RENT OR BUY?

If owning your own home is so expensive in the long run (and possibly counterproductive to building wealth), would it not be better to rent and invest the difference? You would also save on maintenance costs and other hidden expenses.

The answer may be yes if we consider financial aspects only, but the decision to own your own home goes much deeper. A home provides financial security both today and in your old age (you cannot be evicted or have your rental increased to the point where it becomes unaffordable), and it can become a legacy to leave to your children. And while it might appear to be cheaper to rent than to buy initially, over the long term it will be cheaper to pay off your own bond and expenses as opposed to renting someone else's property.

Your home can also be a valuable buffer in times of financial crisis. As time goes on, you build up equity in the property. This is basically the difference between the current market value and your outstanding home loan debt. Although you should not use a home loan as an emergency fund, if you do have to borrow money, taking it out of your home loan would be the cheapest way to do so. It's not wise, as you still need to pay this money back, but it can be the lesser of two evils if your back is against the wall.

The reality is that you need a place to live, and the cost of this is probably the single biggest expense in your monthly budget. So, unless you are fortunate enough to be able to afford a rental property plus a primary residence, or rent a home while investing elsewhere, the clever thing to do is to own the home you live in – no doubt about it.

In the short term, as with any other type of investment, there can be market corrections, as we experienced in the 2008/09 recession. People who bought property before 2008 may have found themselves a few years later in a situation where the property was worth less than what they owed on it. The only thing to do in such circumstances is to sit tight and ride out the storm – as long as it's temporary and not a complete collapse, as happened in the United States with the subprime crisis, which had disastrous consequences for many people.

THE UNITED STATES SUBPRIME CRISIS OF 2008

The 2008 subprime crisis in the United States turned the traditional view of a house being an asset on its head. Overnight, people's homes became liabilities that resulted in financial ruin for both homeowners and the banks that had lent them the money to purchase properties that had become worthless.

Prior to the crisis, house prices in the United States had been increasing steadily for decades, fuelled by increasing demand. Mortgages were freely available and consumers – particularly those with a shaky credit history – were encouraged to buy property, as home ownership was seen as the manifestation of the American Dream. Different types of loans were made available to make home ownership easier, such as interest-adjustable and interest-free loans. These are known as subprime mortgages.

With house prices increasing all the time due to supply and demand, homeowners who couldn't afford to pay the mortgage could easily sell the property. There would be enough equity to cover the outstanding mortgage and perhaps make a small profit. But because of their high personal debt levels, homeowners started defaulting in huge numbers – they could simply not afford to pay the mortgages. Property prices started to decline, and homeowners could no longer use the sale of their homes to pay back the amount they owed, as they owed more than the property was worth. The result was bankruptcy for them and foreclosure for the banks. This, in turn, led to huge losses for the lending institutions. Some couldn't weather the storm. One casualty was Lehman Brothers, the fourth-largest bank in the United States at the time, which closed its doors in 2008. Repercussions were felt around the world, even in South Africa, where the property market experienced a correction in about 2009, although ours was not as serious as the United States experience.

So, what can we learn from what happened in the United States? For me, the most important lesson is not to overextend ourselves, which many people tend to do. When we think of a home as an investment, we may take out second or third home loans to improve our property, or use this money for other purposes. Be wary of overcapitalising – spending more on a property than is justified in terms of market value. Eroding your home equity for other reasons is also not very smart.

People also seldom stay in the first home they buy. We tend to buy more expensive homes when we can afford to. But this simply means more debt, higher maintenance costs, higher rates, and so on. We buy property with a higher value, but also incur greater debt and costs to do so. However, it may take a few years before this has a positive impact on our net worth, as the property first needs to increase in value. Every time you sell and buy a new property, you incur transfer and bond registration costs as well, and you can never recoup these. More importantly, you take out a new home loan, probably for a 20-year term, and never pay off your home loan in full. You simply upgrade the liability on one property to a new one, and keep paying. The decision to upgrade our home is seldom driven by rational financial motives, but rather by status or ego.

We explore different investment options (including property investment) in the next chapter. The smart thing to do is not to confuse your primary residence – your home – with your need to invest to grow wealth. There are many investment options. Do not put all your money into your home; rather use it wisely and see how easily you can end up rich!

Chapter 17

Investing: Understanding the basics

> 'When you invest, you are buying a day that you don't have to work.'
>
> *– Aya Laraya*

It is said that the road to hell is paved with good intentions, but the same might be said for the road to wealth. There are many different views on how to go about becoming wealthy. There is no shortage of 'experts', investment options and information to be found on the internet. On social media we are fed advertisements that promise to make us rich and allow us to retire at 40. It's an endless stream of facts and figures, often more confusing than helpful.

Smartwoman is curious. She cuts through the confusion by getting to grips with the fundamental drivers behind making money and growing wealth. Her greatest weapon is knowledge, and yours should be too. Find out as much as you can about investing and what could affect your investment success. Curiosity and a constant thirst for information will lead you on a path to wealth from which you will never look back.

When you invest, you can only grow your wealth in one of two ways – by generating an income from the investment (and reinvesting that), or by the investment increasing in value so that you can sell it for a higher price and make a profit. In some cases, you may be able to do both with one investment – generate an income and make a profit by selling it in future (such as purchasing a property to rent out, or buying shares that pay dividends).

Investment options range from financial instruments to property, to alternative investments such as Krugerrands and art. The different types of investments are known as asset classes, and they deliver varying returns over the years. Where you decide to invest is determined by any number of factors – how much you know about the asset class, how much money you have to invest, your appetite for risk, whether you are comfortable making your own decisions, and what your goal is. We have already looked at goal setting, and will examine some of these other issues in more detail later. There is no one-size-fits-all approach to investing; you must find the path with which you are most comfortable.

Let's first understand the general principles that apply to investing, irrespective of where you put your money.

SAVING VS. INVESTING

People often use the terms 'saving' and 'investing' interchangeably. Is there a difference?

There are only two things you can do with your money: you can spend it, or you can save or invest it. Spending is easy – you consume goods or services and the money is gone. Saving means putting money aside for some future need. It is a shorter-term approach that offers guaranteed returns and good liquidity. As an example, you may have a savings account at the bank that is your holiday fund – every month you make a deposit in this account towards your annual holiday.

Investing is based on a longer-term view. It includes investing in yourself through your skills and knowledge, with the aim of increasing your overall future wealth. If you invest in your education, for example, you are investing in something that will allow you to earn more money in the future. If you are investing money, the longer time horizon means that you can take more risks, with much greater potential returns. Certain investments may also not be as liquid as money in a savings account.

THE IMPACT OF INFLATION

Inflation has a major impact on our investments, as our money has to work that much harder to ensure that we stay ahead of the pack. We hear about inflation all the time: medical costs are increasing, electricity prices are skyrocketing and life generally seems to keep getting more expensive. Most of us hope that our incomes will increase in line with inflation so that we can keep our heads above water.

Inflation is, quite simply, the devaluation of the purchasing power of money. At the time of writing, inflation in South Africa stood at around 5.2%. Inflation is tracked via a basket of over 400 goods and services. Different people may experience different levels of inflation, depending on what they consume.

We need to make our money work for us, as we have seen. Just as our spending power needs to be able to keep pace with inflation, so our investments not only need to keep up with inflation, but beat it. Then we are making real progress and building wealth.

It is easy to underestimate the impact of inflation, as it happens quietly and builds up slowly. Only when you happen to find an old till slip and see what you paid for items five years ago do you suddenly realise how much prices have increased. It can be quite a shock.

Inflation has averaged around 5.1% over the past ten years. If we assume an average rate of 5%, R10 000 today would be worth only R6 755 in ten years' time, and R3 768 in 20 years' time. So, if inflation remains where it is, our money will lose more than 50% of its buying power over the next 20 years. These are all rough guestimates, as no one knows what the inflation rate will be in reality. Our salaries may seem like a fortune compared to those of our parents' generation, but we can probably afford pretty much the same as they could, if not less.

'REAL' GROWTH

A common term in investment circles is 'real' growth or returns. This is the growth in the value of an investment after taking inflation into account — a measure of how much our money is actually growing. If our money is growing at the same rate as inflation, we are not increasing our overall wealth; we are standing still and there is no real growth.

If we stick to the example of 5% inflation and earn an overall return of 10% on an investment, the real return is 5%. Conversely, if the money invested earns 2.5% growth on it, we are losing 7.5% in buying power – so, we are backpedalling.

It may look simple on paper, but achieving inflation-beating growth on investments is not. Many people are lulled into the security of a fixed-deposit bank account, thinking it is the best decision. It is definitely the *safest* option, but it's not going to make anyone rich. We have to be adventurous and explore other, riskier options. With more risk comes better possible growth, allowing us to create magic with our money and grow our wealth.

INVESTING AS PART OF AN OVERALL FINANCIAL PLAN

Investing and building wealth is part of your overall financial plan and needs to fit in with your other financial needs. Everyone's financial needs and plans differ. To illustrate, let's say that you are a single mother with small children to support. Protecting your income against illness or disability should take priority, before you consider investing.

Your investment plan must be based on your goals. (We discussed goal setting in detail in Chapter 11.) Once you have determined these, you can work out a plan to achieve them. You need to evaluate your plan regularly to see if it's on track, and make changes as needed.

Apart from investing, the other elements of your financial plan should include:
- an emergency fund (the first aspect you should take care of, equivalent to three to six months' take-home pay);
- retirement planning;
- protecting your assets against illness, disability or death;
- medical cover; and
- short-term insurance.

A STRATEGY FOR ACHIEVING YOUR GOALS

Goals are meaningless without strategy. Consider these steps to ensure success:

- Determine your goal and make sure it's realistic.
- Work out how much you need to save each month. If this is not achievable within your budget, you may need to rethink your goal.
- Determine your timeline: how long do you have to achieve this goal?
- Understand how much risk you are comfortable taking.
- Select appropriate investments.
- Document your investment plan, outlining the goal, investment strategy, types of investments and how you will measure your progress.

You may decide to draw up the plan yourself if you are comfortable doing so, or you may want to enlist the help of a professional. We discuss this in more detail in Chapter 23.

RISK AND RETURN

As any gambler knows, the greater the risk, the greater the possible win. Investing is no different: the more risk you take, the greater the possibility of a high return. Conversely, less risky investments offer a lower return.

Investment options are generally positioned on a spectrum of high risk to low risk, starting with equities (shares) at the highest-risk end of the spectrum. This is because share prices fluctuate daily, and there is no guarantee of their increasing or decreasing over time. Also, businesses can go bankrupt, losing all shareholder money. On the low-risk side of the spectrum, you find cash (a fixed-deposit bank account) or corporate bonds, which promise you a fairly low return. It is highly unlikely that you will lose your money, unless the government or business goes bankrupt. Other investment vehicles, such as property, collectibles, unit trusts and gold coins, all have their place on the spectrum. As a rule of thumb, the longer the duration of the investment, the more risk you can afford to take.

Despite their volatility in the shorter term, shares provide good long-term growth, whereas cash provides short-term liquidity (easy access to your money). Both form an important component of any investment portfolio, but often people feel safer putting their money in the bank, particularly when the markets are turbulent.

But you won't get rich keeping your money in a bank account! In 'How to grow your real wealth', a March 2016 moneyweb.co.za article, it was calculated that doubling the real investment value of your money would take nine years if you invested in equities, and 92 years if you invested in cash!

SPREAD YOUR RISK

Accepting and understanding volatility is part of the game of getting rich. It would not be possible without it. Different investments perform at different levels, year on year, and there is no way of picking a winner. Also, you cannot use past performance as a yardstick for future performance. Anything can change, and it usually does. When I first wrote the manuscript for *Smartwoman* in 2017, the top-performing funds over the previous five-year period were in offshore investments. In 2021 this picture is vastly different, with commodities dominating. Who knows which sector will be delivering the top returns in another five years' time?

Some investments are riskier than others; some need more expertise than others. All in all, there is no way of predicting how well any particular investment will do. A diversified portfolio – one that spreads your investment risk across a variety of different investments – gives you the most stable returns, no matter when you need to access your money. It is also very important to have a long-term view: people often get caught up in short-term panic and make the wrong decisions. It takes time to build wealth.

We examine the different types of investments and their performance in more detail in Chapters 19 to 22.

COSTS CAN MAKE A DIFFERENCE

All investments have costs attached to them, and the extent of these costs will affect the final return on your investment.

When you invest in something tangible, such as property, Krugerrands or even art, the costs are easy to see – transfer costs, commissions, insurance, and so on. These must be factored into your cost of purchase.

When you invest in the financial world, costs can be less obvious, but just as critical. If you buy and sell shares, there will be brokerage fees payable as well as other taxes, such as Securities Transfer Tax (SST), Share Trading Transactions Totally Electronic (STRATE), Insider Protection Levy (IPL), VAT, and so on.

To create greater transparency for investors, the Association for Savings and Investment South Africa (ASISA) has developed the Effective Annual Cost (EAC) measure to ensure that consumers are able to compare costs across various investments (unit trusts, long-term savings products, retirement products, living annuities and preservation funds). This overall cost must be disclosed to the investor at quote stage, and includes:

- administration charges – all charges relating to the administration of the investment;
- asset management charges – charges for managing the underlying investment portfolios;
- advice charges – initial and annual fees, both lump-sum and recurring;
- other charges – including termination charges, penalties, loyalty bonuses and smoothing.

Other financial products, such as tracker funds (ETFs), have their own charges, which are generally lower and must also be disclosed upfront.

The return you receive will be after costs have been deducted, so the lower the cost, the more the investment growth paid out to you. Be aware, though, that lower costs are no guarantee of better returns; you need to consider investment return as well. There are a number of financial product providers that heavily promote the fact that they offer low-cost investments. Be very careful before jumping into these; investigate the funds they offer and the expected returns.

PLOUGH BACK YOUR PROFITS

Reinvesting your profits is a powerful lever for fast-tracking the growth of your money. If your investment is generating an income, such as dividends, interest or rental income, you can spend this income or reinvest it and reap the rewards. Manage your investments as if they were a business and see the multiplier effect of your decisions.

GET TIME ON YOUR SIDE

There is no shortcut to building wealth, unless you win the lottery or invent something the world has been waiting for. No matter where you invest, it'll take time to grow. Trying to time the market – to decide when to invest and when to withdraw – can be disastrous, as there is no way of knowing when the best time to do this would be. Patience is critical.

Time benefits investment in many ways. Compound growth, for one, is growth on the initial amount you invest plus growth earned to date. Your money grows exponentially, because you are benefitting from growth on growth. Compound growth can work for you or against you. Albert Einstein is reputed to have said, 'Compound growth is the eighth wonder of the world. He who understands it, earns it. He who doesn't, pays it.'

The Rule of 72 is a quick way of working out how long it will take for your money to double, given a certain growth rate. It's a simple mathematical formula and reasonably accurate for interest rates between 6% and 10%:

Years to double = 72 ÷ Growth rate

So, if your average growth rate is 8%, it will take 72 ÷ 8 = 9 years to double. And at a growth rate of 10%, it will take 72 ÷ 10 = 7.2 years to double.

The magic of compound interest can be clearly seen over time. If you invest R1 000 per month at a growth rate of 10% per annum, compounded monthly, then after roughly seven years your monthly interest will equal your monthly contribution – and this keeps increasing. At 12% growth, your monthly interest will equal your monthly contribution after roughly five and three-quarter years. The earlier you start, the more you benefit from compound growth. It's very difficult to play catch-up.

Let's consider an example. Lisa is 25 and starts investing R1 000 a month. She invests for ten years, then leaves her money to continue growing until age 60. Her twin sister, Jane, also invests R1 000 per month, but only starts at age 35 and keeps investing until age 60. Both earn an average growth of 12% per annum. Who do you think will have more money?

At age 60, Lisa has R4.6 million, even though she only invested for ten years. Jane has R1.9 million, despite having invested for 25 years. There is no substitute for starting early. The difference is the power of compound growth.

INVEST IN WHAT'S REAL

Never invest in something you don't understand or can't see. There are scams around every corner. We dealt with some warning signs in Chapter 14, but it is wise to be vigilant at all times. The smart thing to do is to invest in something that you understand. You will be in a much better position to make informed decisions based on facts instead of hearsay.

The real risk comes in when you hand over your hard-earned cash, trusting that it will be invested well. If you deal with an established financial institution, such as Liberty Life, Old Mutual, Sanlam, Sygnia, Prudential or Allan Gray, you will have a degree of security. These institutions have been around for a long time and have a track record in the form of public information. Make sure that whoever you invest with has been around for a while and has a good track record. There are investment houses in South Africa that have earned an excellent reputation for delivering stellar investment returns. For millions of people, this is the easiest way to invest.

A word of caution, though: always invest your money directly with the financial institution. Do not transfer it into your financial adviser's bank account, as the person advising you is not personally involved in investing your money. Experts within the financial institution do this, so there is no reason for such a transfer. Also make sure that you receive all relevant documentation confirming your investment details directly from the financial institution. I have heard of several tragic cases in which clients paid money into a broker's account, believing it was being invested. Of course, it never was. A financial adviser merely represents a financial services company – they do not invest your money themselves.

As obvious as it may sound, make sure that the company to which you are giving your money actually exists. You must be able to see its offices, find it on the internet and read up on its history. Even this is not foolproof (as we saw in the demise of big financial institutions with long histories, such as Southern Life in the 1990s), but it will go a long way towards protecting you against scammers and fly-by-night companies that offer unbelievable returns.

TAX

You will need to pay tax on income generated from your investments and this will need to be declared in your income tax return. The sale of any investments (like selling shares or disinvesting unit trusts) will also trigger a capital gains tax event. (A summary of tax implications is available in Appendix 4.)

There are numerous types of investment income that have tax implications, at the time of writing:

- **Local interest:** This may be earned from several sources, including saving accounts, Retail Savings Bonds and money market accounts. For people younger than 65, the first R23 800 interest earned is exempt from tax. For people 65 and older, the first R34 500 is exempt.
- **Foreign interest:** This will be earned from offshore investments, and you will need to declare the rand equivalent. You can deduct any foreign tax that you pay and there is no exempt portion for foreign interest.
- **Local dividend income:** Dividends are paid on shares, unit trusts and ETFs. A dividend withholding tax, which is calculated at a flat rate of 20% of dividends earned, is paid directly to the South African Revenue Services (SARS) before the dividend is paid to the investor.
- **Foreign dividend income:** If you earn dividends from offshore investments, these will be taxed. The tax paid on these dividends will depend on the amount and type of shares held in the foreign company.
- **Income from a REIT:** These are treated a bit differently – there is no dividend withholding tax payable. Instead, distributions received from REITs are included in the taxpayer's income and taxed at their marginal tax rate.
- **Capital gain:** This is your 'profit' when you sell an asset, and can include equities, ETFs, properties, Krugerrands, and so on. If you sell your

primary residence, the first R2 million in capital gain is excluded from the calculation. In every tax year, the first R40 000 net capital gain from all your investments is exempt from tax, and for individuals, 40% of the net capital gain is then included in your income for tax purposes. If this sounds confusing, taxtim.com has some really great calculators, including one for capital gains.

You may have heard a lot about tax-free saving plans. These are discussed in more detail in Chapter 22, but the great thing about them is that there is no tax payable on any investment growth or income (dividends, interest, etc.). All gains are for your benefit!

Understanding the tax implications is important when investing, as taxes have an impact on your returns, as do costs. Tax rates may change, so make sure you have the latest information when making investment decisions. Choose your investments carefully and arm yourself with knowledge before parting with your cash. Remember, knowledge is power – grasp it with both hands!

Chapter 18

Investment risk and you

'In investing, what is comfortable is rarely profitable.'

– *Robert Arnott*

So far, you have taken some smart steps to understand your money personality and how this affects your behaviour. You have worked out your budget and set your goals. Now, you can move on to understanding all the investment options available, and how to ensure that you invest according to your level of comfort.

How much of a risk-taker are you? Are you a bit of a gambler, or more conservative? When you make decisions, do you go with your gut, or do you think things through carefully? The answers to these questions will determine where and how you invest, and whether you will be comfortable with your decisions.

Of all the decisions we make in life, we may think that those to do with investing are based primarily on logic. This is far from the truth. Many factors influence our ability to assess information and decide where and how to invest. It's not just about researching the options, but also about knowing ourselves before we jump in, boots and all. Investing is not for the faint-hearted and there are no guarantees (except, of course, in the case of a savings account). You need to understand your own internal drivers and how to make investment decisions with which you are comfortable.

The area of behavioural finance centres on how and why we make financial decisions, and how we can learn from this. Our decisions are not always rational. We use logic, to an extent, but our decisions are often intuitive, based on how our brain has been hard-wired by past experiences.

'EASY' MONEY

I learnt a hard lesson about easy money at age 16. I'd saved up some pocket money for a new pair of sandals, and I walked to the centre of Cape Town on a beautiful summer's day, excited to go shopping and enjoying the feeling of having money in my pocket. My search started on the Grand Parade, where many stalls sold a variety of items. Out of the corner of my eye, I saw some people huddled over a table in great excitement. I ventured closer to investigate. The game was simple – three bottle tops on a board. The game master placed a small stone underneath one of them. Someone would place a bet, and he would shuffle the bottle tops around very quickly. Once he stopped, the gambler would have to guess under which bottle top the stone was. If he was right, he doubled his money. If he was wrong, he lost it all.

I stood mesmerised as I watched the game, my eyes fixed on the lightning-fast hands moving the bottle tops across the board. It didn't seem too difficult – I guessed it correctly a few times – so I volunteered to play. It seemed an easy way to make more money. The stakes were high – each bet was a fixed amount, equal to one-third of the cash I had on me. I handed over the money and it was game on. I won! I was ecstatic. It had been so easy that I bet again. This time, I lost. I played again, fuelled by that feeling of winning and knowing that I could do it – I had managed it the first time, after all.

I lost again. With a sickening knot in my stomach, I bet another third of my savings, hoping to win back some of what I'd lost. But when the shuffling stopped and the bottle top was lifted, I had lost again.

Even as I recall this today, it is not entirely possible for me to describe the intense emotions I felt standing there. The onlookers who had egged me on were not my friends. No one cared that I had lost two-thirds of my precious savings. When it was clear that I no longer wanted to play, the attention shifted to someone else who had shown a willingness to gamble.

I was told afterwards that these games were rigged, which did nothing to ease the utter despair and helplessness I felt in the pit of my stomach. A mere half an hour ago I had been on a shopping expedition, and now I no longer had enough money to buy the sandals. I wandered around aimlessly for a bit, then went home.

I also felt that I had betrayed myself. I had decided to play the game – no one had forced me – and I had been drawn in by the allure of easy money. I didn't blame anyone else. The fact that it had been my own doing actually angered me even more. It haunted me for many months and, to this day, I have no interest in gambling. The loss and disappointment of that very hard lesson has stayed with me all these years, shaping my approach to money and investing, sometimes without me even consciously realising it.

Our past experiences shape us. Often they manifest as a gut feeling. But what about our state of mind at the point of decision-making?

BRAIN POWER

It's almost impossible to separate emotions from decisions. Our state of mind plays a major role in our choices. The more negative we feel, the more we will want to conserve what we have. When we are in high spirits, we may make more daring choices – taking greater financial risk – as the future seems bright and full of promise.

Think about when people are paid a bonus or inherit money unexpectedly. They feel rich, so they spend. It's the ultimate dream for many – to be able to spend without boundaries. This is almost no one's reality, but the euphoria of having extra cash influences our financial decisions. From an investment perspective, a happy mood and a feeling of positivity encourages risk-taking, because it seems like good things will come of the future.

Compare that to someone who has been retrenched and has received a severance package, which they need to invest to provide an income until they find new employment. Their mood and outlook for the future will be very different, and their investment focus will be on conserving and preserving their money, as opposed to risking it for gain.

Avoid making important decisions – financial or otherwise – when an event in your life is affecting your emotions. This is not always practically possible, but it is important to be aware of your emotions and to postpone investment decisions until you are on a more emotionally even keel, if you can.

Another aspect to consider is intelligence. You may be fooled into thinking that only clever people make good investment decisions. This is not true, according to 'Why smart clients do dumb things', a 2016 *Proactive Advisor Magazine* article written by Linda Ferentchak. Ferentchak says that history has shown us that some highly intelligent people have been known to make some really bad decisions. IQ tests generally measure intelligence, but they only measure analytical intelligence – the ability to notice patterns and solve analytical problems. They don't consider other forms of intelligence, such as our ability to deal with novel situations (creative intelligence) or our ability to get things done (practical intelligence). The education system is built largely around analytical intelligence. We often encounter highly intelligent people who are neither creative nor practically minded.

Keith Stanovich, professor of applied psychology at the University of Toronto and author of several books on cognitive behaviour, has found that intelligent people tend to make more mistakes than those of average intellect when solving logic problems, because they tend to take shortcuts or make assumptions. They may be overconfident or undervalue the importance of effort. This, when combined with greed, pride, stress or laziness, results in poor decisions.

Time is an additional issue. We don't always have the luxury of stopping to think. As humankind evolved, certain decisions became 'automated' – our brains recognise patterns and make decisions accordingly. When emotions are involved, we make faster decisions and jump into action. Think of a mother with a newborn baby: when the baby cries, the mother's brain, driven by instinct and emotion, tells her to pick up the baby. She does so automatically, without even thinking about it.

Quick, automatic decisions may be lifesavers when it comes to self-preservation, but if a situation requires rational thought, jumping to conclusions can have the opposite effect.

IRRATIONAL FINANCIAL DECISIONS

Let's return to investment decisions. The study of behavioural finance has come up with many reasons why some people make irrational financial decisions, particularly when it comes to investing. The single biggest reason is that the brain takes shortcuts to avoid having to spend time thinking about decisions.

Our decisions may be biased as a result of the following:

- An aversion to losing: People tend to be more cautious to avoid the pain of losing. People often resist change when they focus on what they are losing, as opposed to what they are gaining. This may be true of my personal example – the pain of losing my money was so great that I didn't want to feel it ever again.
- Basing a decision on a single piece of information (often the first one provided): The first thing the investor hears is the only thing the investor hears. For example, you're told about an investment that a friend has made, one that yielded excellent results. But, your friend adds, it is very risky – there is no guarantee of good returns. You hear only the first part and jump in.
- Basing decisions on what is familiar (past experiences or similar situations): You may take your cue from your parents, or from what has worked for you in the past. I recently met a young man who was about to graduate from university and enter the world of work. When I suggested that he start saving for retirement as soon as possible, he told me that he was going to follow in his father's footsteps and invest in property. He was basing his investment decision on what was familiar within his frame of reference, regardless of whether it suited his personal situation.
- The gambler's belief that patterns repeat and influence future results: Past performance is seldom an indication of future performance, yet some people still believe in following yesterday's winner. Long-term trends are important, not short-term patterns.
- Following the herd: If everyone else is doing it, it must be the right thing to do. This is often the result of clever marketing or hearsay. Celebrity endorsements carry huge weight. They guarantee nothing, but people are still lured into such investments.

How easy is it to overcome these biases? Quite tough, according to Princeton University professor Daniel Kahneman, author of *Thinking, Fast and Slow*. We have two ways of thinking, Kahneman writes. The logical part of our mind analyses problems and comes up with rational answers. This is a slow process that uses a great deal of energy and focus. For example, when someone is asked to solve a difficult problem while walking, they invariably stop so that they can focus on the problem.

The other way we think is intuitive – our gut feel. This is quick and automatic, based on the brain's hard-wiring. Intuitive thinking is based on biases and is so powerful that it is responsible for most of the things we say, do, think and believe. Combined with our emotions, it forms the basis of our financial or economic decisions and is so deep-seated that it is very hard to change, Kahneman argues.

So, our past experiences, emotions, biases and how our brains have been hard-wired to make financial decisions all play a role. It's a highly complicated orchestra with a musical score that differs from person to person. What runs through all investment options, though, is the element of risk. Each type of investment carries the risk of losing money. Some people are more comfortable than others with taking investment risks, and it is important to make investment decisions that you are comfortable with.

Broadly speaking, there are two aspects to be considered when determining someone's risk profile:
- The amount of risk that they can afford to take, considering their income, wealth and investment horizon. The more time they have to invest, the more risk they can take. This is based on cold, hard numbers, and is easy to quantify.
- Their attitude towards risk and the degree of pain they would experience when facing a financial loss – i.e. their tolerance for taking risks. This is less scientific and more difficult to quantify, and is based on past experiences, biases and emotions.

Your risk profile is a critical aspect of any decision about where to invest your money. Your investments must also be structured around meeting your financial goals. There are two options – embark on a do-it-yourself investment plan, or enlist the help of a professional financial adviser or planner. An adviser can take you through a formal risk-assessment process, which indicates what type of investor you are from a risk perspective. There has also been some criticism of this process, however, as it does not always effectively understand personality issues or take them into account.

I did a risk-assessment exercise with a young client who had an investment horizon of over 30 years and earned an excellent salary. The assessment produced the profile of quite an aggressive (that is, high-risk) investor. Yet in my discussions and dealings with her, I came to know her as a very cautious investor who was far from a high risk-taker. Taking this insight into account, I invested her money in a more conservative investment, as she would not have been comfortable with volatile, short-term fluctuations.

If you are dealing with a financial adviser, it is very important that they take your individual perspective and personality issues into account as well. Make sure that the final strategy is one with which you, as the client, are comfortable. Investment decisions cannot be based solely on a few questions in a generic questionnaire.

Consider the following questions when deciding on your investment strategy:

- For how long will you invest the money? Your investment horizon will play a role in how much risk you can take – the longer you invest for, the more risk you can take, as you can ride out short-term fluctuations.
- What is your expected rate of return? The important thing here is to be realistic. If you are not, you won't meet your investment objective. Your expected return will also determine where you could be investing.
- How much of your overall investment does this money represent? In other words, how much risk can you take with this money? Is it your entire investment portfolio? What would happen if you lost it all?
- How much liquidity do you need in this investment? If you have an emergency fund elsewhere and can afford not to touch this money for a length of time, this will have an impact on where you invest your

money (unit trusts, for example, will give you easy access to your money, while investing in a property won't).
- What is your personal risk tolerance? In other words, how much of a loss are you happy to tolerate in the short term to earn more in the long term?
- Which types of investment interest you, and what do you know about or want to learn more about?

We examine the pros and cons of various types of investments in more detail in Chapters 19 to 22, but remember that you need to be comfortable with where your money is invested. Take some time to reflect and ensure that your investment decisions are based on your individual style and preferences. You are unique. Your investment portfolio should reflect this.

Chapter 19

The financial markets made simple

'My mom said to me, "One day you should settle down and marry a rich man." I said, "Mom, I am a rich man."'

– Cher

Understanding how money is made is critical to making smart decisions. The financial markets drive the South African economy and provide the single biggest opportunity for investing and growing wealth. Whether you invest directly or indirectly, most investments are closely linked to the financial markets. South Africa has a thriving financial services industry that allows the ordinary person to access these markets in various ways.

There is a lot of jargon around, though, which can overwhelm and confuse the individual investor. Let's unpack some of the financial industry's terms and phrases, starting with interest rates, which play a major role in regulating the economy and affect investment returns.

INTEREST RATES

It is important to understand how interest rate changes take place, and why. Interest rates are forever going up and down, leaving many people feeling vulnerable to these changes. When interest rates climb, those with interest-bearing investments (mostly pensioners) are happy, and those who owe money (younger people with home loans and other debt) suffer. When they move the other way, sentiments are reversed.

The South African Reserve Bank determines the interest rate and makes changes as it deems fit. As South Africa's central bank, its primary role is to maintain the growth of the country's economy. It does this by maintaining price stability and protecting the value of our currency.

The Reserve Bank uses the repo rate to contain inflation. The repo rate is the rate at which the Reserve Bank lends money to other banks. This affects the rate at which banks lend money to their clients. When South Africans start spending more than they earn and inflation starts increasing, the Reserve Bank may increase the interest rate in an attempt to slow spending down. Interest rates either curb or stimulate spending: the higher the rate, the less people spend, and the lower the rate, the more they spend.

Interest rates play a major role in regulating the economy and affect other investments. For example, when interest rates rise, people have less disposable income, so they spend less. This can affect the profitability of businesses, which, in turn, affects their share prices and perhaps the dividends they pay out. This affects investment returns. Interest rate changes can also affect property prices. Depending on the direction of the interest rate movement, cash investments offering a fixed-interest return could become more or less attractive than other investments. So, changes in the interest rate have a ripple effect across the entire financial market, affecting investments and their returns.

ASSET CLASSES

When people speak about an asset class, they are simply referring to a grouping of similar investments. Different investments within an asset class can have different characteristics and varying degrees of risk, but they all belong to the same basic group. For example, if you invest in a table, a chair, a dressing table and a hat stand, you would be investing in furniture as an asset class.

There are four main asset classes: equities (also known as shares or stocks), fixed-income assets (bonds), cash or money market instruments, and property. These may be local or international. We could also add a fifth asset class – alternative investments, such as gold coins, art and cryptocurrencies. The first four are part of the financial markets. We discuss these in more detail in Chapter 24.

Equities

Investors can buy shares or equities in a company. They then own a small piece of that company. South African shares are generally traded on the Johannesburg Stock Exchange (JSE), the largest stock exchange on the African continent. As of July 2021, 330 companies were listed on the JSE. There is no longer a trading floor, as all trading is done electronically. More than half of the total investments in South Africa are made via the JSE.

Equities can make you money in a number of ways – by increasing in price so that you can sell them in future to make a profit; by yielding an income in the form of dividends that are paid to the shareholders; or even by decreasing in price, if you are investing in derivatives. While many people study equity market trends and movements, there is no guarantee of anything. This is the riskiest of all investments.

If you are investing for growth, there are two types of shares you could consider buying: a growth asset, which you believe will increase in value, or a value asset, because you think it's being sold at a bargain price. These investments are usually suited to people with a longer investment horizon (five years or more). The income they generate is not the main consideration, and there may be short-term fluctuations in their value. Over time, however, they will produce good growth.

Individuals have several options for investing in shares. You can invest via a stockbroker, who will manage your share portfolio for you, advising you about what to buy and sell. Alternatively, you can register an online stockbroking account and make your own decisions. There are investment apps you can use, such as EasyEquities or eToro. You can also invest via exchange-traded funds (ETFs), unit trusts or insurance policies, endowments, and market-linked or other investments with financial services companies. Most insurance companies and asset managers invest a large portion of their clients' money in shares on the JSE, so even by investing indirectly you can still benefit from the growth that the equity market offers. (This is discussed in more detail in Chapter 20.)

Share trading is an extremely complex and risky world. Although some online trading sites will claim to make you an equity trader in a few easy steps and offer the allure of quick money, professional equity traders have years of research and knowledge to draw on and even they still sometimes get it wrong. It takes huge patience and discipline, plus a sound understanding of the market, to be successful. Equity markets are volatile, and novice traders may be confused about whether to buy, sell or hold. They are not for the faint-hearted.

Investing offshore

South Africa represents less than 1% of the world's economy, so investors may be losing out on valuable opportunities by only investing in South African equities. When you invest offshore, you can invest in businesses listed on a foreign stock exchange. This allows you to spread your investment risk across countries and gives you exposure to industries and companies that may not be available locally.

Offshore investments can also be a hedge against a weakening rand. The share price viewed in rands is dependent on two factors: the actual share price and the exchange rate.

You can invest offshore in two ways:

- Direct offshore: Individuals can transfer R1 million out of South Africa per calendar year without needing to obtain a Foreign Tax Clearance Certificate. This includes gifts for people living overseas, online purchases in foreign currency or investing in offshore investments. A further R10 million can be transferred out of the country per calendar year, but you will then need tax clearance from SARS and permission from the South African Reserve Bank. This money needs to be converted into foreign currency and deposited into an offshore bank account, so that you have funds to buy offshore equities. You can buy and sell offshore equities via an offshore share-trading platform, such as that offered by Investec. Apps such as EasyEquities and eToro also have the facility for you to invest in offshore equities, ETFs and exchange-traded notes (ETNs). There is a plethora of options and no personalised advice is given, as these are simply trading platforms. You make your own investment decisions regarding what to buy or sell. This can be daunting for newcomers, and very risky, as you need to do your research well before parting with any money. A number of South African asset managers (such as Allan Gray, Glacier and Sable International) also have investment platforms registered in offshore jurisdictions. These allow investors to access offshore funds that are invested in foreign equities.

- Indirect offshore: With this option, your money doesn't physically leave South Africa. You invest in rands in a local unit trust or ETF that invests offshore via a process called asset swaps. These are offered by all major financial services companies. There is no need for a tax clearance certificate and your investment value is always quoted in rands. It is the easiest way for the average person to tap into offshore investment opportunities. Some of these offshore ETFs and unit trust funds have been top performers over the past five and ten years, delivering growth of around 20% per annum.

Appendix 3 gives you an indication of five-year asset class returns for various global equities. Over the past six to seven years, North American equities have dominated returns, but this situation could change in future. Some funds provide a good balance between North American equities, emerging-market equities and European equities, which offer some diversification to counter the effects of market swings. Do your homework carefully before deciding which offshore funds to invest in. Look at where these funds invest their money – it's possible to invest in Apple or Facebook simply by investing in an offshore fund, whether through rands or through an offshore account.

There are no hard and fast rules about how much you should invest offshore. It is a high-risk investment option, and an investment term of five years or more is generally recommended. If you have an RA or pension fund, up to 30% of this money can be invested offshore in line with Regulation 28 of the Pension Funds Act, so you may already have money invested offshore. When it comes to general investing, a rule of thumb is that between 25% and 50% of your investment could be offshore, depending on how much risk you are prepared to take, and for how long you are looking to invest.

Bonds

When someone invests in bonds, they are lending money to a company or the government for a set period, and are paid a specific interest rate in return. When the bond is issued, it states the interest rate (called a coupon) to be paid, as well as the date on which the bond will be repaid. Interest can be paid out every six months, or it can be reinvested at the same rate. This gives the investor a steady income, paid at regular intervals. The promise to pay the full amount back at a specific date makes this a lower-risk investment than equities.

As soon as bonds are issued, they are bought and sold in a secondary market. Their price is determined by where investors see interest rates moving in future. When interest rates are high, bonds are less attractive and their price is lower. This is because investors can make a better return by investing elsewhere. When interest rates start dropping, demand for bonds increases, so their price increases. Investors can make a profit by selling bonds when interest rates drop. So, they can make money from bonds through the interest they receive, and through the profit they make if they resell them at a higher price.

The bond market is highly complex. Specialised bond traders spend years gaining experience in this space. Bonds are generally bought to be included in institutional investments such as pension funds. Individuals can invest in bonds through bond funds offered by financial services providers such as Allan Gray and Coronation, or the tracker Bond Index Fund from Satrix. You can invest in these funds in the same way as any other fund. They provide diversification at a lower risk, and most have delivered solid long-term returns.

Retail Savings Bonds

In 2004, the National Treasury introduced Retail Savings Bonds to encourage the average South African to save while providing a source of funding for government. Retail Savings Bonds are aimed at individual investors and require a minimum investment of R1 000 (monthly or once-off). You can buy them through the National Treasury, electronically (www.rsaretailbonds.gov.za) or at Pick n Pay or the Post Office. They are fully backed by the government, so your capital is guaranteed. They cannot be resold, but if you need access to your cash before the end of the term, you can make an early withdrawal after 12 months. A penalty will be charged, however. There are no costs in this investment type.

There are two types of Retail Savings Bonds:
- Inflation-Linked Retail Savings Bonds, with maturity at three, five or ten years, and a rate of 2.25 to 4% above inflation (at the time of writing); and
- Fixed-Rate Retail Savings Bonds, with maturity at two, three or five years, and a rate of 6 to 8.5% (at the time of writing), depending on the term.

Interest is paid every six months. In the case of Fixed-Rate Retail Savings Bonds, interest can be reinvested at the same rate, and investors who are older than 60 can elect to have their interest paid monthly (also known as a Pensioner's Bond).

For information about tax payable on Retail Savings Bonds, see Appendix 4 on page 238.

Money market or cash

This asset class includes investments in which you can earn interest, but there is no capital growth. Included here are savings accounts, fixed deposits, bankers' acceptances and corporate commercial papers. Your money remains easy to access, so these investments have high liquidity and are seen as having a lower risk – and a lower return – than equities. They are suitable for risk-averse investors and those who need a temporary holding place while they make longer-term investment decisions. They aim to provide a competitive interest rate, but do not provide significant long-term capital growth.

Again, you can invest in these directly (through a savings account at a bank). Money market investments may be included in some unit trust and financial services market-linked investment portfolios.

For information about tax payable on these investments, see Appendix 4 on page 238.

Property (SA Real Estate)

Property in this case refers to investment in property that generates income through rent and the appreciation of the value of the building without physically owning or managing the 'bricks and mortar'. REITs (real estate investment trusts) are registered on the JSE, and investors can access these by either buying REIT shares (as they would any other share), investing in a property unit trust fund or through a property index tracker fund (ETF). These vary in focus from industrial to residential property markets. They have traditionally delivered strong long-term returns (over ten years or more), and could be an important component of your investment portfolio when building long term-wealth.

WHAT IS THE BEST ASSET CLASS TO INVEST IN?

This is always the million-dollar question, and there is no short answer to it. As stated earlier, spreading your risk is very important for growing overall wealth. There is no way of knowing which type of investment will deliver the best results, and figures change from year to year. You also need to consider your time horizon when selecting investments. If you look at Appendix 1, which shows local asset class returns over one year, you will see that there is no clear pattern as to which asset class performs best over this time period. Appendix 2, which shows performance over a five-year period, indicates that the SA Real Estate class has provided the highest returns from 2008 to 2014, after which it started slipping and global equities rose to the fore. Trends come and go. Powerful market forces swing the odds in favour of various asset classes over time.

With hindsight, we always have perfect vision. However, it is critical to remember that past performance is no guarantee of future performance. This is why it is always a smart idea to diversify – to invest in a variety of asset classes – as this will ensure a better overall return. Some asset classes perform better than others over time, and by diversifying, you will spread your risk. The old adage of not putting all your eggs in one basket holds true.

The same principle applies to offshore investing. Appendix 3 shows global asset class returns over a five-year period. Again, no clear pattern emerges, and investing part of your funds offshore can be part of your diversification strategy. There is no right or wrong when it comes to selecting an asset class. Your time frame and investment objectives are important, and diversification plays an important role in generating good long-term returns.

THE VOLATILITY OF FINANCIAL MARKETS

Because financial markets are so volatile, they often cause panic among investors, who run scared when markets drop and seek more stable investments, such as a money market investment, which offers a fixed rate of return.

When equity markets drop, people sometimes talk about losing money when, in fact, it is merely the value of their investment that has dropped. They only see the real value of their money when they need to withdraw it. At any other time, investments are just numbers. The important thing to remember is that, as truly as markets drop, they recover. History has proven this.

Time is invaluable when you invest in equities. Because of market volatility, they are generally not good for shorter-term investments (less than three years), but over the long term they deliver solid growth. You can see this in the 20-year view of the Johannesburg Stock Exchange All Share Index from August 2001 to August 2021:

JSE All Share Index 2001–2021

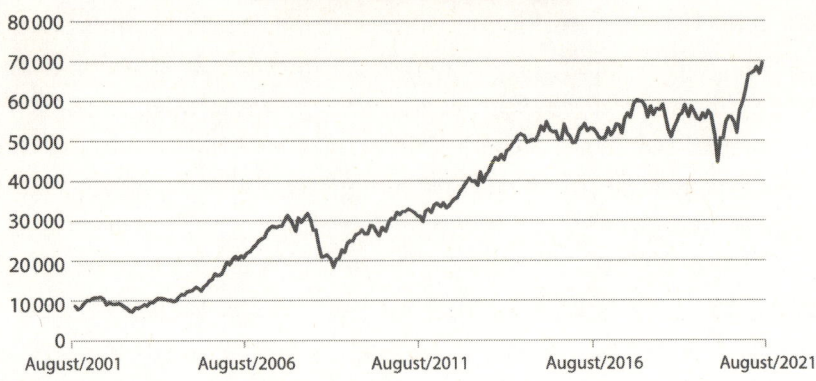

Source: Prudential Investment Managers

The impact of the 'COVID crash' in March 2020 is clearly visible: worldwide markets took a steep downward turn as countries started locking down to curtail the spread of COVID-19. The South Africa All Share Index followed suit but, surprisingly, recovered faster than the indices in the United States or the United Kingdom. Any dramatic drop is nerve-racking for an investor, but the graph tells the story: markets drop and recover, so short-term panic needs to be managed in favour of long-term growth. There has generally been positive growth over any period of five years or longer. Over a 10-year period (till end July 2021), the index delivered 11.6% growth, and over a 20-year period, 14.43% growth (before taking inflation into account and with dividends reinvested). Inflation over the same period was 4.98% (10 years) and 5.39% (20 years).

So, riding out the highs and the lows is a must for anyone who invests in the equity market. This is a long-term investment; running scared and investing in money market accounts instead will deliver disappointing returns by comparison.

RAND COST AVERAGING

Another important aspect of financial market volatility is that it gives regular investors a great advantage: at lower prices, your regular investment can buy more. This is called rand cost averaging. When prices are low, it's bargain time, as any wise investor knows.

The price you pay is an important consideration in any investment. If you invest a lump sum at a low price, you can make a profit later by selling for a higher price. However, there is no accurate way to time the market to ensure that you buy in at a good price.

Instead of investing a lump sum at once, you can use it to make small but regular investments. Or, if you can only afford to invest a small amount each month, you can be sure of getting the best average price over a period. This removes a lot of the emotion and fear from investing. Short-term fluctuations become far less important, as you are investing over time. If there is a recession, or the markets drop, you simply buy more shares or units. If the market picks up, you buy fewer. Averaged over a period, you end up getting the best deal.

Let's look at an example. Assume that you are investing R500 a month in a unit trust investment and the price fluctuates monthly:

Month	Investment	Unit price	Units bought
January	R500.00	R28.70	17.42
February	R500.00	R31.60	15.82
March	R500.00	R31.00	16.13
April	R500.00	R30.30	16.50
May	R500.00	R32.20	15.53
June	R500.00	R34.00	14.71
Total units bought			96.11
Total invested			R3 000.00
Average cost			R31.30
Current value (R34 x 96.11)			R3 267.74

By investing a regular amount each month, your investment gains more value after six months than it would have had you invested at a fixed price and hoped that the price would increase. This example uses a very short time horizon – six months – to illustrate the point. The longer the time horizon, the greater the benefit.

Chapter 20

Investing in equities

> 'I will tell you the secret to getting rich on Wall Street. You try to be greedy when others are fearful. And you try to be fearful when others are greedy.'
>
> – *Warren Buffett*

Equities – or shares – create long-term wealth. They are an important component of any investment portfolio. There are many ways to access the equity market – from buying and selling shares directly, to using professionals to guide and advise you. Many financial institutions (life assurance companies, asset managers and banks) also offer investment options that make it easier for the average person to invest, removing the need for in-depth understanding and experience. The experts do the work for you.

INVESTING DIRECTLY VIA SHARE TRADING

If you want to invest directly, you can do so through a stockbroker or directly online. With over 300 businesses listed on the JSE, there is a wide choice between private companies and commodities. The latter comprises the South African mining industry, and includes gold, platinum, coal and other commodities. You can also invest in property via real estate investment trusts (REITs), as mentioned in the previous chapter. I discuss REITs in more detail in Chapter 21.

Some companies pay a share of their profits to investors in the form of dividends. Reinvesting dividends leads to even greater growth.

Investors are spoilt for choice, but with so many shares to choose from, you can easily make mistakes and suffer serious financial losses. If you are an expert in a particular industry, take advantage of that expertise to identify trends and understand the industry's future potential. If a particular type of investment interests you, do your homework and learn as much as possible about it. Investing is never easy, but your chances of success are better when you are swimming in familiar waters.

If you are new to investing, you could consider investing in exchange-traded funds (ETFs), which will give you exposure to top South African companies. You buy and sell these in the same way as other shares.

Once you feel more comfortable and have built up some knowledge and experience, you may want to start buying and selling individual shares. Many of the online share-trading websites offer courses and ongoing educational information. Some even offer a practice function, where you can buy and sell shares with dummy money. There are also some excellent newsletters and courses available.

Apps have become very popular in this area, including EasyEquities, which is great for newcomers. These apps allow you to trade on global markets. Through eToro, users can invest in cryptocurrencies, stocks, ETFs, currencies, indices and commodities around the world. The UK-based app IG allows South African investors to trade both locally and internationally. If you are keen to get hands-on, then download a few of the apps and see which one works best for you.

Brokerage fees are paid on your transactions and these differ from site to site. Be aware, too, that the smaller your trades, the higher your costs may be proportionally.

I cannot talk about investing in equities without mentioning Warren Buffett. Whenever I speak about him, I always quote his (apparent) first rule of investing: 'Never lose money.' And then, his second rule: 'Never forget rule number one!'

Hundreds of articles and books have been written about his investment strategies. Here are some of the popular ones:
- **Buy at a bargain price.** Buffett believes in buying shares below their market value, and looks for companies that generate lots of cash and have had a consistent operating history for the past ten years.

- **Be patient and wait for the right time to buy.** Market turbulence may mean that shares of great companies become available at a good price, so buy them then.
- **Don't follow the crowd.** Be fearful when others are greedy and greedy when others are fearful. This can make you money.
- **Invest in what you know.** Stick to the industries you understand. If you don't understand a company, or how it makes money, avoid it.
- **When you buy a share, plan to hold it forever.** This means that you are not trying to time the market. Instead, you are prepared to sit tight until you can make a profit.
- **The best moves are usually boring.** Investing is not a path to getting rich quickly. Invest in companies that have proven their worth over time instead of chasing those that may currently be winning in an emerging industry.
- **Buy shares in companies with a competitive advantage.** If there are high barriers to entry for a company's competitors, such as high capital costs, a strong brand identity or patent protection, then shares in the company will be a good investment.
- **Be self-confident in your decisions and don't look for affirmation from others.**

Share trading directly on the JSE carries a very high risk. You should not embark on it unless you have some knowledge and a plan in place. Consider doing a trading course or reading books such as *How to Make Money on the Stock Exchange* by Ross Larter. Be sure to do your homework so that you understand the mechanics of trading and can make informed decisions. Start small, using your spare cash. Do not gamble with money you cannot afford to lose: unless you really know what you are doing, the chances are good that you will lose some or all of it.

WHAT KIND OF RETURN CAN YOU EXPECT?

If we look at five-year intervals of the JSE All Share Index for the past 20 years (to July 2021), we can see that equities have consistently beaten inflation and delivered solid, real returns. These numbers assume that dividends have been reinvested. It is important, also, to remember that this is an index, which shows the movement of the South African equity market. Your actual return will be determined by where you invest, whether in a tracker fund or in individual shares. Some will perform better than others. The following table gives average returns for the JSE All Share Index as at 31 July 2021.

Average returns on investment (five-year intervals)

	Nominal returns	Average inflation rate over the period	Real returns
5 years	8.75%	4.24%	4.51%
10 years	11.60%	4.98%	6.62%
15 years	11.51%	5.61%	5.9%
20 years	14.43%	5.39%	9.04%

Source: Prudential Investment Managers

For information about personal income tax payable on equity investments, see Appendix 4 on page 238.

The pros and cons of trading directly on the JSE

Pros	Cons
• You can grow your capital over time. • Dividends are an excellent source of passive income that you can reinvest if you wish. • You have high liquidity – you can sell your shares easily. • It is easy to invest, and flexible in that you decide how much to invest where – you have full control over where your money is invested. • You can use the professional expertise of a stockbroker.	• It is a high-risk investment and you could lose everything. • You need a great deal of knowledge to trade effectively and grow your wealth. • Dividends are unpredictable. • It may take some time for your investment to grow. • You may need to be fairly hands-on to monitor your investments and make decisions to maximise your return.

EXCHANGE-TRADED FUNDS

A less risky way to invest directly in equities is through ETFs. These funds (also known as tracker funds) track a group (or index) of shares, bonds or commodities, so instead of buying individual shares in all the top 40 companies listed on the JSE, for example, you buy a Top 40 ETF.

An ETF is known as a passive fund, as no one is actively involved in managing it. Market makers take care of all the investment decisions. Using the Top 40 example again, if one company falls off the Top 40 list and a new company enters, the price of the ETF is unaffected and the holdings are adjusted to ensure that the new company is included in the Top 40. Because an ETF is not actively managed, there is no portfolio manager to charge fees, so costs are generally lower. Stockbroking fees, however, are charged on buying and selling, as with any other share-trading transaction.

Investors can buy and sell ETFs like ordinary shares, through a stockbroker or an ETF provider, and you own the share (as opposed to owning units in a unit trust investment). As with shares, their prices fluctuate throughout the day.

The fund does not attempt to beat any benchmarks or outperform any other index. It simply aims to replicate its own performance.

What kind of return can you expect?

Some ETFs have delivered excellent returns over the past five to ten years. Here are the top five performing funds over the past five and ten years (as at 31 July 2021) – assuming that dividends have been reinvested and before inflation has been taken into account. Resources dominated over the past five years and offshore investments over the ten-year period, at the time of writing, but this can't be guaranteed in future.

Top five performing funds over five and ten years (July 2021)

	Fund name	Returns (annualised) before inflation	Average inflation rate over the period
Five years			4.24%
1	InvestRhodium	99.19%	
2	New Gold Palladium	30.98%	
3	Invest Palladium	30.87%	
4	Satrix RESI 10	21.16%	
5	Sygnia Itrix MSCI USA	15.35%	
Ten years			4.98%
1	Sygnia Itrix MSCI USA	23.65%	
2	Sygnia Itrix MSCI/World	19.79%	
3	Sygnia Itrix MSCI Japan	14.55%	
4	Sygnia Capped Indi	14.02%	
5	Sygnia Itrix Eurostoxx 50	13.59%	

Source: etfSA

For information about personal income tax payable, see Appendix 4 on page 238.

The pros and cons of investing through an ETF

Pros	Cons
• Provides a diversified investment compared to buying only one type of share. • You do not need a great deal of knowledge or research to decide which shares to buy. • High liquidity – you can sell ETFs easily, like any other share. • It may pay dividends. • Well regulated by the JSE and Financial Sector Conduct Authority (FSCA). • Costs are generally lower when compared to unit trusts or other investments offered by financial services companies.	• The ruling price of ETFs can vary greatly in line with market volatility. • If you invest a lump sum, you will not benefit from rand cost averaging. • You may not be comfortable with the world of online share trading, or it may seem too complex.

UNIT TRUSTS

Unit trusts are another way of investing in equities. There is a wide selection available in South Africa. You access unit trust investments through investment management companies, financial institutions and banks. You can buy them through a broker or financial adviser, or directly online. Direct investment may incur lower fees, as there is no advice fee payable to a broker or financial adviser. Find out what the various fees are before you make a final decision.

A unit trust is a basket of different financial instruments – such as equities, bonds, cash and listed property – that are combined to make up a specific fund. Individual investors' money is pooled and invested. So, the investment happens in a group, as opposed to each person investing individually.

A fund manager runs the unit trust fund (known as an active fund), with the aim to increase the fund's value over time. They do this by buying and selling the financial assets that make up the unit trust portfolio through the JSE. A fund manager may cost money (that investors ultimately have to pay), but a good fund manager can enhance the performance of a unit trust through good share selection, or defensive behaviour if they are concerned about market conditions.

Individual investors do not own any of the shares in the fund – the combined value of all the shares in a particular fund is split equally to work out a 'unit' price. Individual investors then buy 'units' at the prevailing price (called the net asset value).

When the shares pay dividends, these are paid into the unit trust fund and, in turn, to investors at a predetermined date. You can usually select to have any dividends paid in cash to you or to be reinvested.

The number of unit trust funds has grown exponentially over the past 20 years. Many specialise in a sector, such as the financial sector, the industrial sector or commodities (mining). There are also many general funds. The sheer number of funds means that, in some cases, fund managers are investing in the same assets, making it difficult for the investor to distinguish between funds.

What kind of return can you expect?

As with any other investment, you can expect a wide range of returns. The best-performing unit trust funds have delivered a return of close to 30% per annum over a five-year period, and close to 20% over a 20-year period. Again, resources dominated over the five-year period and offshore investments over the ten-year period at the time of writing. Here are the top-performing unit trust funds over the past five and ten years (as at 31 July 2021), assuming that dividends were reinvested:

Top-performing unit trust funds over the past five and ten years (July 2021)

	Fund name	Returns (annualised) before inflation	Average inflation rate over the period
Five years			4.24%
1	Coronation Resources P	28.81%	
2	IP Global Momentum Equity A	27.76%	
3	SIM Resources	26.72%	
4	Ninety One Commodity R	25.01%	
5	Nedgroup Investments Mining and Resources R	23.83%	
Ten years			4.98%
1	Old Mutual Global Equity R	21.22%	
2	Ninety One Global Franchise FF A	18.68%	
3	Nedgroup Invest Global Equity FF A	18.48%	
4	Allan Gray Orbis Equity FF	18.23%	
5	Coronation Global Opportunity Equity [ZAR] FF	18.14%	

Source: Morningstar

The pros and cons of investing via unit trusts

Pros	Cons
• You can invest a relatively small amount of money, once-off or monthly. • Minimum investment amounts differ from one unit trust company to another. • Unit trusts are easy to buy and sell. • The fund is professionally managed. • It is regulated by the FSCA. • It is easy to keep track of your investment performance online.	• It can be overwhelming to decide where to invest, as there is too much choice. • Fees vary greatly and can affect your investment returns; understand the fees you will be paying. • The unit price is not guaranteed; it fluctuates in line with market conditions. • If you invest a lump sum, you will not benefit from rand cost averaging.

For information about personal income tax payable, see Appendix 4 on page 238.

* * *

Equity investments carry a high risk, and returns can vary widely. There is no way of predicting where to invest. It's human nature to follow yesterday's winners, but past performance is no indication of future performance. Equities should form a significant part of your overall investment portfolio, as they will build long-term wealth. How you access the market is your decision – directly, through ETFs, unit trusts, or through investment plans from financial services companies. These companies offer millions of people the opportunity to benefit from the growth of equities. Often, they will combine equities with other asset classes to provide a range of investment portfolios that carry varying degrees of risk. The return that these portfolios deliver is determined by the fund composition and the portfolio manager's skill in managing the fund.

Please check your investment returns on a regular basis. I am saddened when I see funds that have delivered very poor results over a long period, as I know that people have money invested in them. Any equity-linked investment is a long-term commitment, so do not panic if over a period of a year or less there is no great growth (or maybe even a loss, if the fund is very volatile). But over a period of at least two years or more, you should be seeing upward movement. Keep your eye on your money and evaluate progress on a regular basis – at least once a year.

Chapter 21

Investing in property

> 'Landlords grow rich in their sleep.'
> – *John Stuart Mill*

Investing in property is an important aspect of growing your wealth, as it can provide valuable diversification in your investment portfolio. It also provides stability and solid growth over the very long term (around 20 years or more). According to the South African house price index, over the past 20 years (at the time of writing) property prices have increased by 3.4% above inflation. In the last 10 and 15 years, there has been negative real growth (i.e. after inflation is taken into account) in property prices.

There are several avenues available if you want to invest in property. Some people may believe that owning their own home is an investment. Although it may be an investment in security and family well-being, it will not grow your wealth significantly in the long term because of all the costs involved. It is a high-cost exercise, with rates, maintenance, interest and so on, adding to the expenses. To build wealth, property investment needs to take place outside of your home.

REAL ESTATE INVESTMENT TRUSTS

This is one way to invest in property without owning bricks and mortar. If you don't want the hassle of being hands-on, you can invest via a real estate investment trust (REIT). A REIT is a company that manages a portfolio of properties, such as shopping centres, office parks or residential units. Examples of these companies include Hyprop Investments,

Fairvest Property Holdings, Growthpoint Properties and Emira Property Fund. They are listed on the JSE. You can buy REIT shares just as you would any other share, through a stockbroking website, and you pay stockbroking fees.

Rental income is generated from these properties and, once all expenses have been deducted (such as rates and taxes, electricity, maintenance, etc.), as well as the cost of financing, the surplus is paid to shareholders as a dividend. Because the rental income is based on long-term rentals, you have a fairly predictable income stream. In addition, rentals increase with inflation, so your income (dividend) is fairly inflation-proof.

Apart from a regular income, these investments also offer possible long-term growth through the increase in the share price. The Property Index (which consists mostly of companies with a REIT structure) dominated South African asset class five-year returns up to about 2017, but has battled to maintain this position in recent years. It has been largely overtaken by global equities, as you can see in Appendix 2.

The pros and cons of investing in REITs

Pros	Cons
• You get indirect exposure to a wide range of expertly managed properties. • The rental or lease agreements mean that you get a regular income stream that increases annually. • You get exposure to immovable property without huge capital outlays. • They are more liquid than investing directly in property, as they are traded on the JSE. • They are well regulated, not only by the rules of the JSE, but also by the Companies Act, the Collective Investment Schemes Control Act and other relevant legislation.	• Falling occupancy rates and other market forces can affect their revenue. • The share price is directly affected by movements in the property market, so a downturn will influence REITs negatively. • Rising interest rates will negatively affect profitability.

For information about personal income tax payable, see Appendix 4 on page 238.

* * *

If you do not want to invest directly in the stock market but still want to benefit from diversification in property, then consider the many ETFs, unit trusts and long-term market-linked investments that offer a property portfolio and include REITs in their fund composition.

If you want to be more hands-on with a property investment, you can always consider purchasing a rental property. Using the bank's money to generate an income and grow your wealth is a really smart thing to do.

INVESTING IN RENTAL PROPERTY

Investors make money from property by buying low and selling high. If you buy cash or if you hold on to an investment property until the bond is paid off, you can then use the rental income to supplement your income. Many people have done this as part of their retirement planning – investing in a rental property (or several) with the aim of paying it off by the time they reach retirement age.

There are two metrics when evaluating the viability of a property investment: the growth in the value of the asset and the yield. If a property is purchased cash, calculating the yield is a simple calculation:

Gross yield = annual income ÷ purchase price X 100

Let's say you purchased a property for R850 000. Transfer costs would amount to around R23 200, so the total investment is R873 200. Rental income is R7 000 per month (R84 000 per annum).

Gross yield = R84 000 ÷ R873 200 X 100 = 9.61%

But investors have to take into account the ongoing costs of maintaining a rental property, so a more accurate measurement is the net yield:

Net yield = annual income less expenses ÷ purchase price X 100

Assuming that you pay R900 a month on levies and rates, and a further R300 a month for maintenance and repairs, your rental income per annum is now R45 600 after expenses have been deducted.

Net yield = R45 600 ÷ R700 000 X 100 = 6.42%

The yield gives you an indication of your return on investment. If the property is financed with a bond, the calculation is a bit more complex. Additional costs (such as bond registration costs) will add another R52 500 to the purchase price, so the total cost of the property is now R902 500. Let's say you invested R202 500 in cash, to cover the costs and a deposit of R150 000. You would need a bond of R700 000, which will cost you R5 427 per month at 7% interest over 20 years. Your rental income would now be only R373 per month (R4 476 per annum), which is the R7 000 rent less levy, maintenance and bond repayment. To calculate gross yield, divide the annual return (R4 476) by the initial cash that you invested (R202 500) and times 100:

Gross yield: R4 476 ÷ R202 500 X 100 = 2.21%

These calculations should be done on an annual basis, taking the capital appreciation of the property into account, which would be added to the cash investment you have made (R202 500 in this example). A professional property practitioner will be able to assist in the calculations so that you make an informed decision.

Property is a long-term investment: you need to be able to ride out the high and lows (and there are many) in order to make a decent profit.

The first property most of us own is our home. It provides stability and a host of other benefits. It does not necessarily add to your long-term wealth, but if you make smart decisions it can lead you to a position of owning rental property.

For most people, the first home they buy is not the one that they will stay in for the rest of their lives. As people's careers progress and they earn more, they tend to sell and buy bigger, better homes. This is not the wisest move if you are trying to build your wealth.

How about an alternative – smart – option? You will have some equity in your property and may even be able to rent it out at a rate that covers your home loan and other costs. Buy a second property to live in, and use some of the equity from home number one (if necessary) to pay transfer fees or a deposit. Then rent out home number one and get the full benefit of property investment – an asset that appreciates in value but doesn't cost you a cent!

This type of investment revolves around using the bank's money to grow your own long-term wealth. Let the bank finance your new home, and use your rental income to help secure the loan. You will have to prove rental income by means of a signed rental agreement. You may not be able to afford the big, elaborate house you desire as your second property, but if you buy cleverly and let your first property pay for itself, you should be able to sell it in a few years at a handsome profit and put that money towards a bigger home. Then, rent out home number two. If you can afford to, as your income increases, invest in further rental properties.

The other option is to purchase a rental property as your first property. Property is expensive and it can be difficult for young people to get their foot in the door. Everyone should strive towards owning their own home, so it is smart to get into the property market as soon as possible, even if it means buying a small flat with a friend and renting it out.

You need to fully understand the financial implications of purchasing an investment property. The first aspect is the additional costs you will incur, including:

- transfer duty – at the time of writing, transfer duty is only payable on properties over R1 000 000;
- bond registration costs;
- property transfer costs; and
- miscellaneous costs – new carpets, maintenance jobs that may need to be completed before anyone can move in, etc.

Property24.com has an easy-to-use calculator that will give you an indication of the costs of bond registration and transfer. You will need cash for these, unless a bank is prepared to provide finance for this aspect. Note that this rarely happens. You may also need to pay a deposit if you cannot secure a 100% home loan. You will need cash for this, too.

Shop around when applying for financing, as banks will offer different interest rates. You can use a bond originator or apply on your own – it's very easy through most bank websites – although multiple credit applications may have an adverse effect on your credit score.

An important aspect to consider is your cash flow. You will need to pay monthly expenses such as bond repayment, rates, levies and maintenance. Your rental income may or may not be sufficient to cover these costs. You may therefore need to subsidise the property initially. The larger your deposit, the lower your bond repayments. This will help you get the numbers to balance. Ideally your rental income would cover all your monthly expenses, but bear in mind that you can only charge a realistic rental amount. Do your homework thoroughly to calculate how much you will need to pay in monthly. You should break even after about 24 to 36 months, assuming annual rental increases.

Good tenants are crucial to the success of owning rental property. You can use a professional rental agent (which will add to your monthly expenses), or you can procure and manage your own tenant, which I personally do. It all depends on how hands-on you want to be. All potential tenants should be screened. Screening includes checking their track record and credit history to make sure they can afford the rent. Make sure you maintain the rental property regularly, as this will keep overall maintenance costs down. It's much cheaper to fix a small problem immediately; if you neglect it, it can turn into a major, costly issue.

Traditionally, landlords have escalated rental amounts on an annual basis, but over the past two years, rental property vacancy rates have increased dramatically, as many people had to cancel their rental contracts as a result of a number of factors, including the financial impact of COVID-19. At one point, around one in ten rental properties were vacant on average across South Africa. Many landlords have therefore kept rental amounts level for some time. Some have even reduced theirs to attract tenants. An empty investment property costs money every day it stands vacant, so a good tenant is like gold.

Being a landlord carries a high level of risk, particularly when the economy is tight and there is more stock available than potential tenants.

Also, when interest rates rise, you cannot automatically increase your rent to cover this extra cost. The same holds true for any other cost, such as an increase in levies or rates. You need to have an appetite for being a landlord and must have a buffer of money for times when you have no rental income.

How good an investment is property really, though? The South African house price index is an average. Across the country, there are areas that outperform the index, and others that underperform relative to the index. Also, trends come and go as to which type of properties are more in demand than others. There are currently a number of growing niche markets: mixed-use developments, retirement complexes, student accommodation offering a live–play–work lifestyle, and lock-up-and-go properties for retirees. Mixed-use developments in growth or business nodes or in the heart of the city provide a lock-up-and-go lifestyle for people close to work.

Tips from an expert

Owning a rental property can be disastrous if you don't know what you're doing. It's a hands-on investment, so make sure that you do your homework upfront. Samuel Seeff, chairman of the Seeff Property Group, says that you need to consider the following eight golden rules when you decide which rental property to buy:

- 'Location, location, location' is as true today as it has always been. Understand the area in which you are considering buying, do research, speak to agents operating in the area and make an informed decision.
- Investigate the neighbourhood thoroughly, and ensure that there are good roads, services and fibre connectivity.
- Check out the street or complex to make sure that your property is in a good position relative to other properties. Compare other prices to make sure you are not paying more than you should be.
- Do not pay more than the property is worth, unless you are 100% sure that you won't have to sell the property before it reaches market value. Remember, too, that property price growth follows economic growth closely; if the economy stalls, so will property prices.

- The better the facilities, the more in demand a property is likely to be. Transport facilities, shops and schools all make the property more attractive to potential tenants and future buyers.
- Security is an important issue today. The more secure a neighbourhood is, the more attractive it will be for tenants and buyers. Find out whether there is a neighbourhood watch and what type of security the property has.
- If you are investing in a holiday rental, then leisure facilities and nearby attractions such as the beach or a river are important. Put yourself in the shoes of anyone wanting to rent the property – what would attract them to come and rent there?
- Find out what other landlords are charging in the area so that you can budget for any shortfalls. Also make sure that you have a buffer in your budget to cater for any hidden costs that may arise (such as unexpected maintenance).

The pros and cons of rental property

Pros	Cons
- The investment pays for itself. Once it breaks even, it starts paying you an income. - It provides diversification against a downturn in the equity market. - Through capital growth, it allows you leverage that you can use to purchase additional properties. - It is a tangible investment and is easier to understand than some other investments. - Most expenses related to the property are tax deductible.	- There are high entry and exit costs, such as transfer fees, estate agent fees, etc. - You need a financial buffer against tenants not paying rent and major unexpected repairs. - It can take up to three years before you break even in terms of cash flow. - You cannot liquidate it easily if you need access to cash in a hurry. - You need to be actively involved in managing your property and tenants – which takes up your time. - Interest rate increases can affect you negatively.

TAX IMPLICATIONS OF RENTAL PROPERTY

You will be taxed on the income generated from rental property. This includes income from renting holiday homes, bed-and-breakfasts, guest-houses, subletting a room in your house or renting a whole property to a tenant. This income is added to your overall income for tax purposes. Money such as refundable deposits is not included in your taxable income, as long as it is placed in a trust account.

Expenses incurred in generating this income – rates and taxes, interest on your home loan, advertisements, repairs and maintenance, estate agents' fees, levies, and so on – are deductible from your income.

If you sell any of your properties at a profit, the capital gain will be added to your taxable income. At the time of writing, the first R40 000 per tax year is exempt, and on your primary residence the first R2 million capital gain is exempt.

* * *

There are many options when it comes to investing in property. Choose the one with which you are most comfortable. Invest in a property fund or a REIT if you want a hands-off investment; if you have the time, money and desire to get your hands dirty, invest in rental property. It can be a great investment, and also a lot of fun.

Chapter 22

Investing through financial services companies

'Money is only a tool. It will take you wherever you wish, but it will not replace you as the driver.'

– Ayn Rand

Another easy and popular way of accessing the equity market and other high-performing investments is through the variety of investment options and plans that the financial services industry provides. Some claim to specialise in certain fields (such as wealth management), while others offer investment plans for specific reasons (such as an education plan). All in all, they operate in the same basic way – they invest your money in a range of portfolios or funds, which differ in their composition to appeal to different investors. Like unit trusts, these funds are actively managed by a fund manager who aims to match and beat industry performance benchmarks.

They can contain any mix of assets and are structured to provide a wide range of risk-and-return profiles. Most allow for a lump sum or a monthly investment. They are usually sold by brokers and financial advisers who earn fees for the advice they have rendered to you.

Banks traditionally offer a variety of fixed-interest savings accounts, as well as longer-term investments from other financial institutions, which are sometimes co-branded.

TAX-FREE SAVINGS PLANS

Tax-free savings plans were introduced in South Africa on 1 March 2015 to encourage South Africans to save. Their main benefit is that there is no tax payable on any interest or dividends earned on the investment, regardless of how long you invest for, and there is no tax payable when you withdraw your money.

You can currently invest up to R36 000 per annum in a tax-free savings plan, with a lifetime limit of R500 000, which includes the total investment across various companies. So, you can have more than one tax-free savings plan, but if you invest more than R36 000 annually, or more than R500 000 over your lifetime, you will pay a penalty of 40% on the additional amount. You declare your contributions to tax-free savings plans as part of the annual tax return that you submit to SARS.

There are also restrictions on where your money can be invested. For example, it cannot be invested in funds in which fees are based on performance or in funds that keep some of the proceeds back from investors (such as smoothed bonus funds). You have easy access to your money and cannot be charged a penalty for this.

Tax-free savings plans are available through banks, unit trust funds, asset managers and long-term insurance companies. Banks give you a predetermined interest rate, so you know what your return will be. Asset managers and long-term insurance companies offer growth based on the performance of the fund in which you invest. The banks all offer different interest rates, terms and minimum investment amounts. Shop around before you decide where to invest, based on your timeline, investment goals and appetite for risk. Get advice from a professional financial adviser if you feel you need to. Alternatively, you can buy many of these products online.

The pros and cons of tax-free savings plans

Pros	Cons
• A tax-free savings plan can be taken out as a gift for a child by a grandparent or parent. • It has a minimum investment of R50 per month through a bank account, which encourages saving, no matter how small. • It is a disciplined way of saving or investing. • You can invest with low-risk options. • If SARS does not require you to submit a tax return, you will not benefit from the tax deductibility of RA contributions, so you may benefit from a tax-free savings plan instead. • It offers a high degree of liquidity (it will be easy to access your money without incurring penalties).	• Many investors are well below their threshold for paying tax on interest or capital gains anyway, so this is not a unique advantage. • Contributions are not tax deductible, so if you are investing for the long term, an RA is probably a better deal, as your contributions will be tax deductible. • The plan is not protected from creditors. • You have easy access to your money, which means you will not achieve your long-term savings goals unless you are disciplined.

INVESTMENT PLANS

Traditionally offered by long-term insurance companies, these plans are either sold as investment plans or packaged for a specific need, such as education funding. Your money is invested in funds that match your risk profile and time horizon, and these funds are unitised, so they are very similar to unit trusts. The value of your investment depends on the unit price at any given time. Fund fact sheets are available so that you can see the fund's objectives, historical performance and composition.

Some investment plans are subject to Section 54 of the Long-term Insurance Act of 1998, which places restrictions on accessing your money within the first five years, and on the amount by which you may increase your premiums. The more modern, unit-linked investments are transparent and centred on client needs. They have no restrictions on withdrawals and are extremely flexible. Nevertheless, always make sure you understand the investment's terms and restrictions before you commit to it.

A great benefit of investing with a long-term insurance company is that you can add a premium protection benefit for death, disability, or both, depending on the investment. This ensures that the investment will continue as planned, even if you become disabled or die.

Let's say you are investing to provide for your child's tertiary education needs. You could then add premium protection so that even if you die or become disabled before your child reaches university age, you can be sure the funds will still be available. Or, if you are saving for retirement, adding a disability premium protector ensures that your premiums will continue to be paid until retirement age, even if you are disabled before the time. Your investment goals will thereby remain secure.

You can also add beneficiaries to these investments, so that the proceeds pay out directly to them in the event of your death, and not into your estate. This results in a saving on executors' fees. In some instances, you can also add a beneficiary for ownership so that, upon your death, the investment is passed on to someone else, who continues with it. The investment does not stop and pay out, as would be the case if you nominated that person as a beneficiary. For information about tax payable, see Appendix 4 on page 238.

The pros and cons of investment plans

Pros	Cons
• With premium protection, you can ensure that your investment goals are secure, even if you become disabled or die. • They provide a disciplined way of investing. • You have easy access to your money, depending on which option you choose. • You can nominate beneficiaries to have the proceeds paid directly to someone, and not into your estate. • They can be used as security. • Some offer excellent returns, as they contain a large portion of equities in their fund composition.	• These plans can be costly, as there may be advice and other fees payable. • They are rigid if they fall within the realm of the Long-term Insurance Act. • There are no guarantees, so they could be subject to short-term volatility.

RETIREMENT ANNUITIES

No one likes paying tax, so here's a smart option that can save you tax! A retirement annuity (RA) is specifically designed to provide you with funds at retirement. Irrespective of whether you have employer-provided retirement benefits (a pension or provident fund), an RA is a highly tax-efficient way of ensuring a comfortable retirement.

Long-term insurance companies and unit trust companies offer RAs. Specific tax implications differentiate RAs from other long-term investments. These are specified by the Income Tax Act, which has changed in this regard in recent years.

Investments in RAs are geared towards retirement, so you cannot access your funds before you are 55 years old. If you stop contributing before you reach retirement age, your money will remain where it is and continue to grow until you reach retirement. You cannot take a loan out against an RA. It is safe from creditors, and cannot be attached if your business is liquidated or you declare insolvency.

If you are investing in an RA, there are rules governing where your money is invested to protect your retirement savings. In terms of Regulation 28 of the Pension Funds Act, no more that 75% of the fund may be invested in equities, no more than 30% may be invested offshore, no more than 25% may be invested in property, and no more than 10% may be invested in hedge funds. These rules have been put in place to ensure that retirement savings are not invested in high-risk assets, because of the importance of retirement funding.

In 2021, draft legislation was tabled by National Treasury that will allow retirement funds to invest up to 45% of the money they manage in infrastructure, such as bridges, roads, cellphone towers, etc. This investment will be optional.

The most important advantage of RAs lies in tax implications for the investor – while you are contributing and building up your retirement nest egg, as well as when you reach retirement age and need to access your capital.

TAX IMPLICATIONS OF RETIREMENT SAVINGS

Your contributions towards retirement savings are tax deductible, up to certain limits. For many years, there were two separate calculations for deductions – one for your pension fund and one for RAs. From 1 March 2016, this all changed as part of the South African government's retirement reform process, a process aimed at encouraging South Africans to save more towards retirement.

In essence, all contributions to your pension fund, provident fund and RAs – whether they are made by yourself or your employer – are tax deductible up to 27.5% of the higher of your remuneration or your taxable income before deductions. There is an overall maximum contribution limit of R350 000 per annum.

What does this tax deduction mean? It simply means that your taxable income is reduced by the amount you are contributing. Your taxable income decreases, so you pay less tax. The smart thing to do is to plough this extra money into your retirement savings, making your money work even harder for you. You can also make a lump-sum injection should you receive a bonus or other windfall.

Some employers will take your RA contribution into account and adjust your tax deduction accordingly. Many will not do this, though, nor will they take any of your ad hoc lump-sum injections into account. So, when you do your tax return, you should be pleasantly surprised with a nice refund. Again, the smart thing to do is to plough any refund back into your RA as an ad hoc lump sum, so you get a direct benefit from the tax advantage. Also, you will be able to include this as a tax-deductible contribution in the next tax year, rolling the benefit forward!

If you are self-employed, your RAs will be the basis for calculating the tax benefit. For this reason, self-employed people, together with their accountants, often work out how much extra they can contribute in terms of the tax benefits around January each year, and then make a lump-sum investment before the end of February.

You can access the funds in your RA at age 55 at the earliest. You can take one-third in cash. The first R500 000 is taxed at 0% at the time of writing, and the balance is taxed at a preferential rate, according to the retirement tax table. All lump sums you have received over your lifetime are added together for this tax calculation. So, if you received cash as severance pay, for example, or as part of your pension or provident fund as well as your RA, the first R500 000 of the total is taxed at 0%. The monthly income you receive in the form of a pension will be taxable according to the individual income tax tables.

The pros and cons of an RA

Pros	Cons
• Contributions reduce your tax liability. The more you save, the less tax you pay. • No tax is payable on the investment's growth. • Retirement savings are protected against insolvency. • There are favourable tax rates at retirement. • You can make lump-sum injections. • It is a disciplined, structured way to save for retirement.	• You cannot access funds before age 55. • Only one-third may be taken as cash at retirement. • It can be costly, as there may be advice and other fees payable.

Weighing up which investment option is the best for you can be daunting. Your choice will depend on how involved you want to be, how much knowledge you have and how willing you are to pay for advice. Paying for advice could be the best thing that you do, because the world of investing can be complex. It's easy to get lost if you don't have an expert at your side or do a course to understand how to invest directly. The bottom line is the return that you receive.

Speaking of advice: you can get it traditionally by interacting with a person, or you can get it from a machine – the so-called robo-adviser.

Chapter 23

Advice: Man or machine?

> 'I don't believe in that term "self-made" – not to be offensive, but I believe everything happens for a reason, every single person you meet. Even if it's one single person giving you advice, that person helped you get to where you're at today.'
>
> *– Michelle Phan*

Being smart means doing what is right for you. You work hard for your money; decisions on where to invest it should not be taken lightly. The world of money is fraught with jargon, and it may feel as if the only people who understand it are those who work in that world!

The easiest option is often just to put your money into a bank account: it's simple to understand and you know what return you will receive. But, as you know by now, this is not the path to wealth. You have to get a little more daring, take a little more risk. This often means more complexity, and the stakes are higher. Apart from the jargon, there are many choices. You may also believe you need lots of money to make more money, that the barriers to entry are high and that investing is only for the rich. This is not true. But unless you know what you are doing, it's easy to make mistakes. You may either make your investment decisions yourself, or you may prefer to get advice.

Once you get guidance from a professional financial adviser, you may experience a great feeling of security and comfort in handing your money over to an established financial services company and then waiting for your money to grow. After all, advisers are the experts, right? Well, yes, they are, but this comfort comes at a cost: you will pay for their advice, which will impact on the overall cost of the investment. Fees will always be charged, no matter where and how you invest. They will just vary depending on the type of investment.

There is a growing body of people who want to control their own investment decisions. I call them DIY investors. You can invest directly in the JSE and make your own investment decisions, as we have discussed. But if you want guidance on where to invest, you are going to need advice from a person or – perhaps – a machine!

THE ROBO-ADVISER

The technology that has transformed so many everyday things – shopping, communication, education – has now moved into the realm of investment. In 2008, in the midst of the American financial crisis, the first robo-adviser was developed. It has been refined over the years, and today investment advice is within everyone's reach.

A robo-adviser is a computer program that calculates where you should be investing and recommends a portfolio that will help you achieve your investment goals. If you are making your own investment decisions and selecting which funds to invest in, you are not using a robo-adviser. A robo-adviser will lead you through a series of questions about your assets and liabilities, risk profile, investment timeline, personal circumstances and goals. You need to understand the risk assessment questions – they are not always simple to someone who is not in the financial services industry – and answer them correctly. Based on your answers, the robo-adviser designs an investment portfolio around your profile in a process similar to the one that human advisers use, but they rely entirely on technology. The portfolio is made up of equities, bonds and money market investments, as well as ETFs.

A number of robo-advisers are available in South Africa, including through OUTvest, Nedgroup Investments, Sygnia and ABSA. They can also be found on sites where you can invest in unit trusts directly online.

Once you have invested, the algorithms continue to work for you, monitoring the markets, recommending switches if doing so will benefit you, and generally managing your portfolio. This is something that a flesh-and-blood adviser may not actively do, as it is time-consuming and virtually impossible to micromanage each client's account. Technology is perfectly suited to this.

Investing in this way is simple and transparent. You can see how much it is costing you, and you can access your investments at any stage to check their performance. Most also allow you easy access to your money, which means good liquidity (although this is not a unique feature). It can also save you costs, as there is no advice fee, and other fees are reduced, too. This can have a significant impact on your investment return after a number of years.

There are also no biases or mistakes, as technology has no emotion and no agenda. Based on cold, hard facts, it's always objective, and it's appealing to the young, tech-savvy investor. Its ease of use attracts people who may not otherwise have taken the trouble to see an adviser and who may just have put their money in a bank account.

Some investors prefer the reassurance of a human being, however, and value the relationship that they form with their adviser. In an industry based largely on trust, not all investors trust a computer. It can be quite a mindset shift to take advice from one, particularly for the older generation!

Bear in mind that robo-advice is not suitable for problem-solving. It cannot consider your holistic financial situation, or any existing investments or planning that you have in place. It cannot interact with you and probe you for relevant information that you glossed over or forgot to mention. It cannot draw up a complete financial or retirement plan, look at your lifestyle and income protection, or take tax and similar issues into account. It also cannot advise you about life-changing events such as divorce or the death of a spouse, so its use is very limited. To date, there is no proof that investment plans structured by robo-advisers have delivered better returns than those structured the old-fashioned way.

If you need a quick, simple, cost-effective investment plan, though, then by all means take this route. Just be aware that it works within a set range of portfolios and investment options, and if you need anything more, you will need advice from a human being.

If you are shopping around for the right robo-adviser, here are some questions you may consider asking:
- Is the minimum investment amount in line with what you can spend? They seem to range from R500 per month or a single premium of R10 000.
- Are the services offered purely online, or will you have access to a financial adviser if you need more complex advice?
- What are the fees? Lower fees were a driver in the development of robo-advisers.
- What information do you need to supply, and how do you change it? The information you provide affects your investment results directly, so it is important to know how much time you have for changing your input data and whether there is online support in case you don't understand a question. It may be useful to play around with the tool if you can, to get a feel for what will be required of you.
- Which economic guidelines and assumptions do they use (such as the inflation rate)? Read the fine print to make sure that this is in line with your expectations.
- Will other services be provided as your financial needs become more complex? Your initial investment needs might be simple, but you may need advice about tax, retirement planning, estate planning, and more, as time goes on. Can a robo-adviser provide this?
- How do you terminate your contract, and how long does it take to terminate? How long will it take to get your cash out? If it is a retirement investment, can you transfer the funds to another retirement account?
- How will your personal data be protected? This is critical in the world of hacking and phishing. Find out whether the service shares your data with third parties and how you can opt out of this.

You can also combine your robo-adviser investment plan with advice from a face-to-face adviser, with your investment portfolio forming part of your overall financial plan. The two are not mutually exclusive – they can work together very well.

Over time, the range of robo-advisers' services may expand. But since we do not make investment decisions in isolation from the rest of our lives, we might still have a great need for financial advice in the future. I am not convinced that computers will ever be able to meet that need completely.

USING THE SERVICES OF A FINANCIAL ADVISER

Money is about life and life is about people, and for generations the financial services industry has been built on relationships. If you wanted information or advice about investing, insurance or any other aspect of financial planning, you would turn to a financial adviser. Whether it's an independent broker, a bank broker or a family member who becomes our go-to person, our natural tendency is to seek advice from someone we both trust and perceive as an expert.

Years back I knew a financial adviser who lived and worked in Verulam, near Durban. She was so entrenched in the community that, as soon as young people in the community started their first job, their parents would send them straight to her 'to take out a policy'. This struck me as a wonderful philosophy for parents to have – to get their children to start saving from the first month in which they started earning a salary.

This example also illustrates the respect people had for her as an adviser. One cannot emphasise the value of these relationships enough. Good financial advisers fulfil a role that goes far beyond managing your money. They take the time to get to know you, understand your circumstances and take an interest in all aspects related to your financial well-being – your net worth, your income, your dreams and goals, your fears and your bad habits (such as spending too much) – and they will advise you about the steps you personally need to take to achieve your goals.

Another very important consideration is your stage of life – where you are in your life cycle and how this affects your financial planning. A single career woman, for example, will have very different financial needs from a married woman in her fifties. Investing and financial planning is not a one-size-fits-all solution; when you work with a financial adviser or broker, you get a tailor-made plan.

The process of financial planning is a lifelong road that you travel with your adviser, a financial coach, mentor and expert in their field. But what is the actual value of this advice? According to the Investment Funds Institute of Canada, research and academic studies have confirmed that people who use advisers on an ongoing basis have better savings habits and achieve higher levels of wealth than those who do not. They are also more confident that they will be able to meet their retirement needs.

Unfortunately, not everyone sees financial advisers in this rosy light. There are horror stories about bad financial advisers, leading to distrust and scepticism of the industry. As is human nature, the bad stories spread like wildfire, while the good stories remain largely untold.

In South Africa, the financial services industry has undergone many changes over the years. Legislation has made the industry more professional, transparent and protective of consumers' rights. Advisers need to be qualified, declared to be 'fit and proper', and follow a strict advice process that is transparent and protects the consumer. No amount of legislation, though, can ensure a comfortable relationship with an adviser, or build your trust in that person. People sometimes ask me where they can find a good adviser, and I always suggest that they speak to friends and associates to find a referral. A friend may have dealt with someone they would like to recommend, but there's no guarantee that this recommendation will work for you. It may be useful to also ask why your friend is referring this particular adviser. Good reasons may be that the adviser provides outstanding service, or explains everything clearly. If your friend recommends the adviser because they doubled your friend's money in a year, however, be wary – this is too good to be true, and you don't want to deal with fly-by-night advisers (or anyone else who promises you astronomical investment returns).

When you finally meet the adviser, you need to feel comfortable with that person, and to like them. We all prefer to do business with people we like. First impressions count. If your gut feel tells you that something is not right, walk away. There are plenty of advisers out there. You will find the right person.

Apart from trusting your instincts, remember that all financial advisers must be registered with the Financial Sector Conduct Authority (FSCA).

There are also some questions you could ask potential advisers to get a sense of whether they would be a good fit for you:
- How long have they been in the industry, and what are their qualifications?
- Which companies do they deal with? Are they only mandated to sell one company's products, or do they sell products from companies across the spectrum? Ideally you would want to deal with an independent financial adviser who can offer products from a range of companies so that you get the best deal, as opposed to an adviser who can only sell one company's products, and is, in fact, an employee of the company.
- What process do they follow when providing advice? They should follow a thorough, six-step process that ensures that all aspects of your situation have been considered when they compile your financial plan (we discuss this process a little later in this chapter). If not, the warning bells should start ringing.
- Who do they work for, and is there back-up if they are not available?
- How often will you meet? You should meet at least annually to review your financial plan, but a good adviser will meet with you more frequently.
- How do they earn their income? Do they earn commission based on products that they sell, or in a fee-based system? In future, clients may be able to cancel the ongoing advisory fee if they feel that their adviser is not delivering a good service.

Generally, advisers follow a six-step process when they give you advice and compile your plan:
- **Step 1:** The initial discussion, in which the financial adviser finds out about you – your dreams, concerns, family situation, needs, and so on. The adviser should also outline the process they will follow and how they will be remunerated, and then obtain your consent to continue.
- **Step 2:** The adviser gathers information about your goals, timeline, existing provision and investments, and any other information that will play a role in achieving your goals.

- **Step 3:** The adviser analyses your financial data to formulate a plan to achieve your goals.
- **Step 4:** The adviser presents their recommendations to you. These may contain different scenarios based on different rates of return or time horizons. You should receive the plan in writing, as well as a written record of the advice.
- **Step 5:** You give the adviser your permission to implement the plan, assuming that you are happy with everything. If not, the plan is amended and presented to you again, before you authorise its implementation.
- **Step 6:** The ongoing monitoring of the plan. As your life and circumstances change, or markets change, your plan may need to be reviewed. Your adviser will do this with you on a regular basis (at least once a year) as part of their continued service to you.

Some advisers charge a flat fee for drafting the financial plan and then the client can implement the plan themselves. This may be prohibitive to many clients, as the cost of drawing up a comprehensive financial plan can amount to a good few thousand rand. The bulk of advisers don't charge for the financial plan but earn fees based on the investment that the client makes. This can be up to a 3% initial advice fee and between 0.5% and 1.5% as an ongoing fee.

Your financial plan will not only cover investments but provide you with a holistic financial picture, including advice and recommendations for protecting your income or your family's financial well-being in the event of illness or death.

How do you decide between getting advice from a machine and dealing with a traditional financial adviser?

Some people prefer a more DIY approach to investing, whether it's via a website or an app; others may prefer to deal with a person. If you're not sure which route to follow, the next table gives you some indication of which type of adviser might best suit your needs. While by no means foolproof, circle either 'yes' or 'no', and then tally up your selections to get an idea of where your preference may lie. Before you make any decisions, though, I encourage you to do some research and speak to friends who may have experienced both types of advice. Make an informed decision and do what feels right for you.

	Robo-adviser	Financial adviser
I am happy to invest without any human contact	Yes	No
If markets drop and my investment is negatively affected, I'm happy not to discuss it with anyone	Yes	No
I am comfortable with doing business transactions online	Yes	No
I fully understand the impact of fees on my investment performance	Yes	No
I am happy to be hands-off and let someone else make all my investment decisions, both in the beginning and over time	Yes	No
I understand the automated process and agree with the investment allocations made by the robo-adviser	Yes	No
My only need is investing – I don't need advice about any other aspects such as retirement or estate planning	Yes	No

Chapter 24

Kruger to crypto – alternative investments

'Not all that glitters is gold; not all that is sticky is tar.'
— ***Lithuanian proverb***

Not all investments yield an income. There are some fun alternatives that are more tangible than the traditional financial market options. These include investing in gold coins, art, rare furniture and even diamonds. The value of these investments lies in the growth they offer and the profit you can make when you sell them.

And then there are the 'new kids on the block' – cryptocurrencies – which have been touted as the solution to all the evils of the traditional financial world, and the way of the future. There are heated debates around the value of cryptocurrencies as an investment or as an actual currency that can be used to pay for goods. Many people have polarised views. However, it's worth including these alternatives in the chapter, as my gut feel is that they are going to be around for some time and the battles will continue raging. But let's start the discussion on alternative investments with something more traditional – Krugerrands.

KRUGERRANDS

By far the most popular form of gold coin worldwide is the Krugerrand. This is a direct investment in gold, and its price is determined by the gold price in US dollars and the US dollar/rand exchange rate. Because of this, Krugerrands can be a good hedge against inflation, falling exchange rates and general uncertainty in the South African economy.

Krugerrands were introduced in 1967 and are all minted in South Africa. There are other gold coins available, but Krugerrands remain the most widely held and traded gold bullion. Each coin is made of 22 carat gold. They come in four sizes: 1 ounce, ½ ounce, ¼ ounce and ¹⁄₁₀ ounce. About 60 million have been sold worldwide.

You don't need any special knowledge or experience when buying or selling Krugerrands. You only need to understand the implications of owning them, and make sure that they are kept safe – obviously, they can be stolen.

Krugerrands are available from certain banks and specialist bullion dealers, such as The Scoin Shop or Mr Kruger. There is also an app, Isa-Gold, which you can download to buy and sell Krugerrands. You'll pay a commission of between 7% and 12% when you buy a Krugerrand, so shop around to get the best deal. Krugerrands are not a short-term investment – you need to wait for their price to go up substantially before you sell them if you want to make a profit.

Investing in Krugerrands diversifies your portfolio. Gold is a good hedge against a weakening currency and, as a non-renewable resource, it has a positive track record of returns. Over time, the price of Krugerrands has increased steadily, making them excellent gifts for a newborn child, perhaps as an endowment for when the child reaches adulthood.

To illustrate the power of this investment, let's take an example of a one-ounce Krugerrand bought at the end of June 2000 for R1 980. Ten years later, in June 2010, it was worth R10 000, and by June 2020, R34 000. By July 2021, the value had dropped back to R28 200, but it will no doubt climb again. If its value had only kept pace with inflation from June 2000, it should have been worth R5 979 in July 2021, so the growth in its value well exceeded inflation over the 21-year period.

Investing in Krugerrands means that your investment is not dependent on the performance of any particular gold mine. Krugerrands also often perform in the opposite direction to other asset classes, so they are a good portfolio diversifier.

If you don't want to invest directly in gold but still want the benefit of this commodity, you can invest through an ETF that specialises in this metal. This may also be a cheaper option.

DIAMONDS

It is said that diamonds are a girl's best friend, but there is a vast difference between buying diamonds to wear and buying diamonds as an investment. Investing in diamonds is far more complex. You need to understand the four Cs that give a diamond its value: cut, clarity, colour and carat. Unless you know what you're doing, you would be well advised to work with an expert in the field.

In the case of gold, an overall price determines the value of your investment. Diamonds work very differently: a good investment is a diamond that will appreciate faster than other diamonds over time. Each diamond is unique. Advisers generally recommend investing in diamonds that are larger than one carat, with flawless clarity. However, some coloured diamonds, such as yellow, blue and red, also make excellent investments.

Investing in diamonds is complex and not for the average person. Returns are made over the medium to longer term. You need to have the best expertise and be connected to the right experts and networks to maximise your investment. Failing this, stick to buying diamonds for adornment, and focus your energy elsewhere in your pursuit of wealth.

ART, RARE FURNITURE AND OTHER COLLECTIBLES

The South African market for art, antiques and rare items has shown remarkable growth in recent years. Paintings, books, stamps, military memorabilia and furniture from the Anglo-Boer War and other Africana are all being snapped up by collectors. They serve a dual purpose: investors can enjoy them and, if they are purchased at a good price and well looked after, they can be an excellent investment.

The value in these items boils down to what someone is prepared to pay for them. As a collector, you should focus on items that interest you. It's probably best to decide on a particular line to invest in and stick to that. The options include art, silverware, antique furniture, stamps and rare glassware. Research the subject thoroughly online and in person by spending time in museums and galleries. Identify popular artists and trends. If you are investing in art, you may also consider doing an online art appreciation course, which some big auction houses offer.

Start small and build up your collection over time. Each time you purchase an item, keep a record of where and when you bought it, as well as any other information about the item. Have it valued and keep a written certificate of this valuation, as well as receipts of all your transactions. This will protect your investment – as will insuring it and taking care of it properly.

If you are buying art, there will be additional costs, such as commissions. These range from 10 to 20% for auction houses, and can be as much as 40 to 50% if bought through a gallery.

In addition to taking out insurance, you need to make sure that you keep it in a safe place where it will not get damaged or stolen. Many items in this category are enjoyed in the investor's home, but be aware that normal wear and tear can devalue an item. Hanging a rare painting above a hot fireplace, for example, could cause the paint to dehydrate and flake.

From an investment perspective, many people believe that art and other collectibles are not as risky as investing in shares, as the former maintain their value and appreciate over time. According to experts, most good-quality art and antiques appreciate at about 10% per annum in the medium to long term, which is a healthy return on investment.

If you want to invest in art without having to buy any, Masterworks (www.masterworks.io) sell shares in iconic artworks as a form of investing. While you don't actually own the painting, you also don't have to store it safely. When Masterworks sells the painting one day, you share in the profit. There is no minimum investment and it is easy to make payments by credit card from South Africa. The company also offers a secondary share market, but this is not available outside of the United States at present.

Art investments may attract tax, depending on whether they are deemed to be for personal use. Consult a tax practitioner for clarity about your personal situation.

CRYPTOCURRENCIES

When you hear someone mention cryptocurrencies, Bitcoin is usually the first name that springs to mind. Originally developed as a decentralised currency around 2009 by a programmer under the pseudonym Satoshi Nakamoto, Bitcoin signalled the start of a new era of blockchain technology and decentralised digital currencies.

Unlike money as we know it in the form of physical cash, cryptocurrencies are virtual or digital money in the form of tokens or 'coins'. They are decentralised, which means that they do not belong to any country or central bank and are developed by teams who build systems to issue them, called 'mining', as well as other controls.

Cryptocurrencies started with Bitcoin, but today there are literally thousands of cryptocurrencies around, including Ethereum, Litecoin, Bitcoin Cash, Ripple, Dogecoin, TRON and Cardano. Fortunes have been made and lost by 'investing' in these cryptocurrencies, as they are highly volatile and risky.

Understanding how the value of these cryptocurrencies is derived is a real challenge to the traditional financial market. When you buy shares in a company, you are buying a piece of a brick-and-mortar business that sells a product or service and generates a cash flow and profits (hopefully). That gives the share its value. The company may pay back dividends (a share of the profit) to shareholders, and the share price will hopefully increase over time as the business grows.

Cryptocurrencies operate completely differently – there is no business, cash flow or profit driving its value. The value is driven by a belief that these will increase in value in future as they are removed from the control of central banks and payments may be more secure than traditional payment systems.

While cryptocurrencies were developed to be a new method of payment, their extreme volatility creates a problem. A currency needs to be stable so that buyers and sellers can determine a fair price for goods and services. If the value of the currency keeps changing, it's near impossible to determine that fair price. To illustrate, one Bitcoin was worth close to $20 000 in December 2017, but a year later it was worth only around $3 200. By December 2020, it was at a record high again.

Prices are also very susceptible to comments from market leaders. In May 2021, a tweet from Elon Musk about suspending purchases using Bitcoin because of the high amount of fossil fuels consumed by mining Bitcoin sent the price tumbling.

I'm not an expert in this area at all, but I am often asked whether it is worthwhile investing in Bitcoin, Ethereum or other cryptocurrencies. I can only consider this from the traditional investment world that I know and understand. My take is that, for the average person, investing in a cryptocurrency is akin to gambling: you have no idea what will turn the odds in your favour. Even for people who have studied the crypto world in detail, there are still too many unknowns. So, if you want to put some money into crypto, let it be money that you are prepared to lose. Most of us don't have money like that, but I believe this is the only way to look at this type of investment. If you can't afford to lose even R1 000, then steer clear of crypto investing.

If you are going to take the plunge, then invest via one of the apps that are available, such a Luno, VALR or eToro. Any capital gain that you make will, however, need to be declared when you do your tax return, as it is subject to taxation.

Also be aware of crypto scams that promise high returns. In 2021 alone, the initiators of two massive crypto scams in South Africa – Mirror Trading International and Africrypt – apparently absconded with around $4 billion in investors' money. These were two of the biggest crypto scams in the world.

Crypto products are not registered with the FSCA, and thus not regulated at the time of writing, but this matter is receiving high priority.

Ultimately, the decision is yours. I don't hold a strong position for or against cryptocurrencies, *but* I think there may be a future for them. Just because we don't understand something within our tried and tested frame of reference doesn't mean it's wrong. But I will repeat my very stern word of caution – if you buy cryptocurrencies, you could lose everything you put in. Investing in crypto cannot be the basis for your long-term investment plan. Use a bit of 'mad money' you can play with if you want to satisfy the gambler in you, but until this world unfolds and we understand it better, stick to the more traditional forms of investing (with a proven track record) as the foundation for your future financial security.

Chapter 25

Protecting your wealth when life throws you off course

> 'A big part of financial freedom is having your heart and mind free from worry about the what-ifs of life.'
>
> *– Suze Orman*

Have you ever considered what your greatest asset is? We tend to measure our wealth by our assets, but the starting point of all of it is our ability to earn money. Without money, we cannot survive, let alone build any kind of wealth. So, if we go right back, our ability to earn money – whether we earn a salary or are self-employed – is our greatest asset. This was brought home very vividly during the COVID-19 pandemic, when lockdowns devastated many industries and saw millions of people worldwide on short pay or with no income due to business closures and job losses.

Protecting your income is a crucial part of creating long-term wealth. Protection means keeping it safe if something goes wrong. When we face a crisis, or some huge, unforeseen expense, having extra money means not having to dip into our hard-earned investments just to keep our heads above water.

This is the role of life assurance and all the other products that fall within this arena. Life can be a bit like a game of roulette. You earn an income that buys you a lifestyle. You use this money to live, build wealth and perhaps leave a legacy for the future. It's great when you are on a winning streak. But you never know what is around the corner – there are a multitude of potential threats to your wealth. We looked at divorce in some detail earlier, but there are other threats, such as illness, disability, retrenchment and death, which affect not only you but your family too.

Being smart means being prepared. We have no way of knowing if or when any of these events will occur in our lives. It is almost impossible for the average person to build up enough wealth to survive these events from a financial perspective. Taking out cover is a bit of a gamble, but so is not taking out cover. You don't know whether you will need it because you can't predict the future.

Often considered a 'grudge purchase', much like car or household insurance, this cover makes people eternally grateful when something goes wrong, as it provides valuable cash in times of crisis.

It is very important to remember that you need to review and adapt the type and value of your cover as your circumstances change. You should do this at least annually.

There are three primary types of cover: life cover, disability cover, and severe illness or trauma cover. Some companies offer retrenchment cover too, which pays you an income for a limited period in the event of retrenchment. This gives you breathing room until you find a new job because it means you don't have to erode the wealth you've built up just to survive from day to day.

COVER FOR WHEN THINGS GO WRONG

Let's look at some of the challenges that life can throw at us – situations that can be financially devastating if we are not prepared.

Retrenchment or early retirement

Retrenchment and early retirement are essentially similar events, except that retrenchment may happen to you at a far younger age than early retirement. Either way, both of them are major threats to the wealth you have accumulated. Without an income, you may quickly start eroding your wealth.

You may have had the foresight to take out retrenchment cover, which should tide you over until you find employment again. However, with an unemployment rate of around 30% in South Africa, work is scarce. Many people decide to start their own small business or find some kind of self-employment. This can seriously affect your long-term wealth, particularly if the business venture fails. Some people are also tempted to cash in their pension fund (or at least a part of it) or other investments that they have accumulated to fund their new business. This can be a tragic mistake. If the business goes under, the money is lost; if it survives, it will still be difficult to make up all the years' worth of growth on those investments.

So, having retrenchment cover and even using the benefits offered by the Unemployment Insurance Fund (UIF) makes good financial sense.

Another word of caution: when money is tight, people tend to cancel their insurance policies. This is short-sighted, as the family loses the policy's cover and security. If, at some point in the future, the family's financial situation improves and they want to take out life cover again, they will probably find that the premium is much higher because they are older than when they took out the initial policy. They may also have developed health issues that make cover more expensive or prevent them from getting cover at all.

As an alternative to cancelling your policies, you may be able to reduce the level of cover and, consequently, your premiums. Check with your insurance company before taking drastic action.

Severe illness

In the wise words of Mahatma Gandhi, your health is your true wealth. One cannot argue with that. Today, life expectancy is far greater than it was a mere hundred years ago, thanks to advances in medical science, better nutrition and vastly improved hygiene.

We may live longer now, but we are plagued by 'lifestyle' diseases – cancer, stroke and heart disease are the big three. There are many other, less prevalent ones too. Contrary to popular belief, these illnesses are not new. The earliest description of cancer (although it was not called by that name) dates back to 3000 BC and was discovered in Egypt. The Edwin Smith Papyrus is a copy of part of an ancient Egyptian textbook on trauma surgery. It describes surgery on tumours of the breast that were removed by cauterisation with a tool called the fire drill. The writer also noted that 'there is no treatment'.

Heart disease was prevalent among the Pharaohs. Egyptian mummies, some as old as 3 500 years, show evidence of heart disease – specifically a narrowing of the arteries, according to researchers who presented their results at the 2009 American Heart Association meeting in Florida. Among those who were plagued with the disease was Pharaoh Merneptah, who died in 1203 BC. Nine of the 16 other mummies they had studied showed the same signs.

According to the Heart Foundation, one in three men and one in four women today is expected to suffer from cardiovascular disease (heart attack or stroke) by the age of 60. And, according to the South African Cancer Society (CANSA), more than 100 000 South Africans are diagnosed with cancer every year. The top female cancers are breast, cervical, colorectal, uterine and lung cancer, and women have a one-in-seven lifetime risk of contracting one of these. The top male cancers are prostate, colorectal, lung, non-Hodgkin's lymphoma and Kaposi sarcoma, and men have a one-in-six lifetime risk of contracting one of these.

These illnesses have been around forever, but their treatment has changed, and many people can survive what might have been certain death in previous generations. Thanks to phenomenal advances in medical science, heart attacks, strokes, cancer and many other dread diseases now have impressive survival rates. This is wonderful news, but the costs associated with illness can be financially crippling and may seriously damage our long-term wealth. The common mindset is to insure ourselves in case we die, but we actually need money in case we *survive* these illnesses. We need to insure ourselves in case we live!

The first weapon of financial survival in the face of severe illness is belonging to a good medical scheme. There are many available in South Africa, offering a variety of benefit options. Most people do not understand the benefits of their scheme, and only read the fine print when they submit a claim and find that the scheme will not pay. It is critical to understand what your medical scheme covers and what it does not. There may be limits for cancer treatment, for example, or it may exclude payment for certain specialised medicines or treatment regimes, which means that you will have to fund these from your own pocket. If you run out of benefits, you may still be able to receive treatment in line with the prescribed minimum benefits (PMBs), which is equivalent to the treatment you can receive in a government hospital.

There is often a difference between what the medical profession charges and the benefits your medical scheme pays. This difference may be substantial. To make up for this shortfall, consider taking out medical aid gap cover, which will ensure that you do not have to find the cash to settle any cost differences.

Medical costs are just one aspect of severe illness. Another is a softer issue: taking time off from work for treatment and recovery. This could be an extended period, depending on the nature of your illness. Chemotherapy, for instance, can last for six months or more, and patients are emotionally and physically drained during this time.

Once you are well enough again, you may want to return to your job, but this may not always be possible. Consider some scenarios. If you work for a small firm, for how long will they keep you on their payroll until you can return to work? Will they give you unpaid leave, or perhaps dismiss you due to ill health? If you are self-employed, no work means no pay, and you will drain your financial reserves just to stay afloat. If you are a homemaker, someone may have to be employed to perform your duties at home and to take care of you, putting strain on the family's resources.

When you are ill, the last thing you want to worry about is money. You also don't want to be forced to sell valuable assets and erode your wealth just to survive. You want to focus all your energy on your treatment and on getting back on your feet instead.

Severe illness cover (also called trauma or critical illness cover) pays out a lump sum, usually one month after diagnosis of your illness. This money is not linked to your medical scheme; you can take out this cover whether you belong to a medical scheme or not. You can use it as you need to – to cover shortfalls, to give yourself the luxury of taking time off work, or even to change your life. I believe that a severe illness is a life-changing event; you look at life differently afterwards. You may not want to return to the stressful lifestyle that led you there. Having cash gives you choices and the opportunity to alter the course of your life.

Over the years, I have given many talks to women on the subject of breast cancer, and of the many stories I have been told, two remain with me always. The first was in East London, from a young woman who had always dreamt of owning her own business. After a divorce, with a two-year-old son to take care of, she shelved the idea and stuck to her day job. A year later, she was diagnosed with breast cancer. She had severe illness cover in place, and the policy paid out. She was able to get good treatment and had fully recovered by the time I met her. She had used the cash payout to cover her medical shortfalls, but also to buy an old container, which she kitted out as a takeaway shop in an industrial area. She realised her dream of owning her own business, despite going through a strange and traumatic set of circumstances. She turned her life around and could spend more time with her young son, while still earning a good living.

The other story was from a woman in Johannesburg who told me, rather shyly, that she had used her severe illness payout to do something she always wanted to do – play bowls in Ireland. An avid bowler, she had often dreamt of making the trip, but financially it had never been possible. Again, through a strange set of circumstances and the foresight of taking out severe illness cover, she found the money to go to Ireland. The trip had been part of her healing – a really wonderful, heart-warming story!

How do you decide which cover to take, and from where? Advice is always valuable, as the options can be confusing and daunting. Different companies offer varying levels of benefits and cover a variety of illnesses. You can also buy cover as a stand-alone policy or add it to an existing life-cover policy.

At one end of the spectrum, you can buy a niche product such as a cancer policy that covers you for certain female cancers (breast, cervical, uterine, etc.) only. At the other, you find policies that cover a wide range of conditions. Between these two points are further options in terms of the level of cover. Some cover is based on severity – the percentage of the benefit it pays out will depend on how far your illness has progressed at diagnosis. You may have cover for R500 000, for example, which will only pay out in full if you are diagnosed at the most severe stage of your illness. Sometimes, the percentages payable per level of illness are specified upfront. At other times, these are decided at the claims stage, depending on the medical information supplied. Make sure you understand when the cover will pay out.

I do not see the benefit of taking out niche products, such as a cancer policy. You can't predict what illness you will get, and the premiums on these policies are often not much lower than those of policies that cover a wide range of conditions. What's the use of a cancer policy if you have a heart attack?

The bottom line is that you need to shop around, get quotes and understand the benefits offered. One last point: people often think that these illnesses only happen when you're older. Yes, the possibility of illness may increase with age, but there are no guarantees. And when you are younger, you have fewer financial reserves to see you through a crisis like severe illness. So, cover is important, even if you are in your twenties. The beauty, of course, is that cover is so much cheaper when you are young. Protect your wealth against illness – it's simply not worth taking a chance and ignoring it.

Disability

In this context, being disabled means that you are unable to work and earn an income due to illness or injury. Disability could severely damage your accumulated wealth. Without financial provision, you have to draw on your resources just to survive. You may not have enough to sustain you for the rest of your life.

Losing a limb or vital part of your body's function, such as your sight, could mean the end of a career and its income. How would you fund your lifestyle? And, more importantly, what effect would this have on your wealth?

Insurance companies offer a variety of disability cover options:
- Any occupation: You are covered if you cannot do any kind of job at all.

- Own or similar occupation: You are covered if you cannot do your own job or a similar one, based on your training and experience.
- Own occupation: You are covered if you can no longer do the same type of work that you are currently doing, which often applies to professionals.
- Cover can also be temporary or permanent. There are waiting periods, and assessing the extent of the disability can take time.

If you have a pension or provident fund through your employer, you may have disability cover (and life cover) included as part of your group benefits. However, if you leave your employer, this will fall away. The older you get, the more expensive it becomes to take out cover. In some instances, there is a conversion option available on leaving the fund, which means that you can take out the equivalent amount of cover in your personal capacity without any medical requirements.

The need for disability cover is heightened if you are self-employed, as no work means no income. Even if you are disabled temporarily (e.g., you suffer an injury that leaves you unable to work for a few weeks), you still need money to live.

Smartwomen protect their wealth while they're building it. They won't have to do so forever – once they have enough wealth and a financial buffer, they can stop paying for cover, as they will be financially secure, no matter what happens.

Chapter 26

The show must go on

'Death is just life's next big adventure.'

– J.K. Rowling

Severe illness and disability are possibilities, but death is a certainty. What does death have to do with building wealth? If you're dead, you're dead, right? You have no need for money. So true, but life cover is not about you; it's about the significant people in your life. We are all part of a family. We may have people who are dependent on us, or we may be dependent on others. Life cover protects us from the financial effects of someone's untimely death.

The death of your spouse or partner could wreak havoc on your financial situation. Apart from the initial expenses, such as medical and funeral costs, there is also the loss of income and the need to maintain the family's standard of living.

If the death follows a long illness, there may well be large unpaid medical expenses. Most medical schemes do not cover all costs, and families are left to foot the bill. Some insurance companies pay out the life cover on a policy before death if the insured patient has a life expectancy of a year or less (in other words, is terminally ill). This can go a long way towards relieving the family's financial burden.

Funeral costs can amount to thousands of rands. Many people choose to have some kind of funeral cover, either through a special funeral policy, or through a benefit added to their life cover. Most companies offer the option of including the immediate family in the policy, and some companies add extended family (such a parents and parents-in-law). Check out the options available to you.

Death can cause other, even greater complications if you or your partner have your own business. If either of you died (or became disabled), how would the business continue, and what impact would it have on your dependants? If your spouse or partner owned the business, what impact would this have on you? People sometimes use their primary residence as security for business loans, leading to an intricate web of business and personal financial interests. An untimely death, when there is not enough cash, can be devastating to those left behind. I have heard stories of widows who had to start working in their late husband's businesses after their death, because he had no life cover and the families depended on the income from these businesses.

Maintaining the family's standard of living is the greatest challenge when someone dies. It is also important to have a will in place.

Some people believe that if you don't have dependants, you don't need life cover. This is not always so simple. A young person starting out in life may not have any dependants, but they may have debt, such as a student loan or other short-term liabilities, that are not covered by credit life insurance. If they died and their liabilities exceeded their assets, they would have died insolvent – a rather nasty legacy to leave.

As mentioned earlier, some creditors may insist that you take out credit life insurance that will settle your outstanding balance if you die and, in some cases, if you become disabled or are retrenched. By law, a credit provider is entitled to insist that you have cover, but it cannot dictate who you buy it from. It is a relatively expensive form of cover, as it is not underwritten (that is, your specific medical condition is not taken into account when the premium is calculated). There have been instances of mis-selling and overcharging in the past. Also, your premium does not fluctuate according to your account balance. It does provide a useful safety net, though, in case of death, disability or retrenchment, and has proved very useful during the COVID-19 pandemic when many people were retrenched.

But let's go back to the young person with no dependants who had a student loan and no credit life cover. Someone would have signed surety for their student loan (usually a parent). If the young person died, their parents would be liable to repay this loan. Where would the cash come from if there was no life cover in place? Deciding whether you need life cover has as much to do with dependants as it has to do with what you own and what you owe. If you have signed surety for someone, it is wise to have some cover in place to ensure that there is cash available to repay the loan in the event of that person's death.

A list of assets and liabilities and a calculation of liquidity on death (that is, how much cash there is in the estate and whether it would cover all debts and expenses) is all you need to ensure peace of mind and make sure that no one will be out of pocket if you die. The net worth worksheet at the end of Chapter 15 can provide you with a good snapshot of your situation if you were to die tomorrow.

You may have life cover through your pension or provident fund. Don't be lulled into a false sense of security, however: if you leave your employer, this benefit will disappear. You may also be considerably older at that stage, so replacing this cover will cost you more.

IF YOU LIVE, WE PAY!

Insurance companies offer different life cover options, ranging from accidental death (and accidental disability) to normal life cover. There is a standard two-year suicide clause in all policies – policies do not pay out in the first two years if the life assured has committed suicide.

Some policies allow you to attach other benefits, such as disability and severe illness cover. Funeral or final expenses cover is a popular version of life cover, as it pays out within 48 hours of death, providing cash at a critical time. Some policies also include a cash-back benefit that pays you cash if you do not claim within a certain number of years. As life cover is often a grudge purchase (you never personally see any benefit from it), this can make the deal a bit sweeter. People tend to let their policies lapse within the first ten years of taking them out, either because of affordability issues or because they find better deals elsewhere. The cash-back concept encourages people to continue paying premiums.

This cash-back bonus is built into the premium you are paying and it must be indicated clearly on the quote. You pay, effectively, for the cover and the cash-back portion separately; it's just packaged in one product. The obvious risk is that, if you do claim on the policy, or stop paying premiums before the cash-back date, you lose all those extra premiums you paid into the investment part of the policy.

Ideally, you should keep your cover and your investments separate, which gives you more control. If the idea of a cash-back appeals to you, do yourself a favour and get a few different quotes for cover with and without a cash-back option, so that you can see what you are actually paying for cover and what is for the cash-back premium. Also understand how the cash-back payout is calculated and make sure you're getting a good deal, one that is better than if you took the money and invested it elsewhere. Remember, everyone is competing for your money. Don't fall for marketing hype that may erode your wealth instead of building it!

When considering life cover, know exactly why you need it so you don't end up wasting money. You can get cover for a specific period only (called term assurance) or for your whole life (called whole life assurance). Term assurance, as the name implies, covers a specific term or period only. Often, you can extend your cover at the end of the term if you want to. An example of term assurance is when you take out a home loan and you need cover in case you pass away before repaying the loan in full.

With whole life assurance, the policy pays out on your death, regardless of when that occurs. For this reason, it is more expensive than term assurance, as it will definitely pay out at some point. Don't waste money on whole life assurance if you only need cover for a specific period.

Also be aware that, when you apply for a home loan, it may be a condition of the loan that you have sufficient life cover. You may be sold a policy that includes disability or even severe illness cover. The policy is ceded to the bank: if you die, become disabled or contract a severe illness, the funds are paid directly into your home loan account. If there is any excess (in other words, if your outstanding loan is less than the benefit that has been paid), you will have to apply to access this money. In the event of your death, it will go into your estate when this is wound up.

If you have sufficient cover elsewhere, you are entitled to use this instead (in a similar way to the credit life insurance arrangement). The bank will probably request that this policy be ceded to it, too, if it is a condition of your loan.

Life changes all the time, and our need for cover changes with it. You may take out life cover when your family is young and they need this financial security. As you age and go into retirement, the life cover may no longer be necessary, or it could be reduced. Reviewing it along with all your other forms of cover should be part of the ongoing financial-planning process.

Buying products off the shelf could mean paying for cover that you don't need, or not getting the cover that you really need. Some products come with lots of bells and whistles to attract customers in a fiercely competitive market. I believe in keeping things simple. In most cases, these add-ons, in the form of wellness programmes, special discounts and other lifestyle-related benefits that companies offer, come at a price. There's no such thing as a free lunch, as the saying goes. This is as certain with financial products as it is with anything else. Shop around and make sure you are getting the best price for your needs. If it's life cover, get the best price for life cover. Don't pay more just because you are offered benefits that you didn't need in the first place. Seek professional advice if necessary.

I personally received some advice that proved to be invaluable many years later. Shortly after getting married, my husband and I purchased our first home. I had life cover as part of my employee benefits at work, and we decided to take out cover on my husband's life too. That way, if anything happened to either of us, our bond would be paid off. My adviser at the time suggested I take out the policy on my husband's life and pay the premium.

As things happened, we divorced some years later. My ex-husband tore up the policy contract in anger, saying that it was immoral that I would benefit from his death, since we were getting divorced. Unbeknown to him, I simply obtained another copy the very next day. The point is that I was in control – it was my policy, and I ensured that it remained in force. I protected my own interests and, in doing so, I ensured that my children had a secure future, no matter what happened to my ex-husband. So it was excellent advice for me to own the policy and pay the premiums, as opposed to my husband doing so, which would have been the default had my adviser not suggested differently.

Of course, you can only insure someone else's life if they agree to it, and there must be an 'insurable interest'. In other words, the person doing the insuring must derive some financial benefit from the insured person that they would lose if the insured person died or became disabled.

One last thought: a valid will is something everyone should have and revisit regularly, as their situation changes. Dying intestate means that your dependants could wait for up to two years for the estate to be wound up. A will can be drafted by a professional (such as an attorney) or through a specialist company offering this service. You can also do it yourself online through www.mywillonline.co.za. or www.smartwill.co.za. Just make sure that your will has been witnessed and is stored in a safe place where your family can find it after your death.

You can nominate beneficiaries on your life cover policies, which means that the proceeds will be paid directly to them on your death, and not into your estate. The benefits here are twofold. First, there will be a saving on executor fees, although the policy will form part of the calculation for estate duty purposes. Second, the money is paid directly to the beneficiaries, which means they don't have to wait for the estate to be wound up before they get access to cash. If you are married in community of property, all joint assets will be frozen on death, leaving any dependants in a perilous position while the estate is being wound up.

Creating and building wealth and living our lives is all one intertwined process. Nothing happens in isolation to the world around us. We are all part of a system of family and community – some are dependent on us, and we are dependent on others. As we grow our wealth and our assets, we need to protect them and ensure that unexpected events do not sap our financial resources.

Protecting our wealth is the smart thing to do. It's as important as building it. By being aware of options and pitfalls, we make sure that we spend our money wisely, not wasting a valuable cent on unnecessary expenses.

Chapter 27

Get smart, get going and get rich

> 'The question isn't who is going to let me; it's who is going to stop me.'
>
> *– Ayn Rand*

I was once asked whether I would rather have money or knowledge. Of course, the right answer is knowledge, because that can lead to money, whereas money on its own is meaningless unless you have knowledge about how to make it work for you.

I started this book by asking why we need a book for women specifically. We fought so hard for equality, and yet we still want to be treated differently? Hardly! It's not about how we want to be treated, but rather about recognising that there are differences between men and women, particularly in the challenges that we face.

As women, we tend to have more people and issues competing for our time and our money than men do. Those who are smart see through this and find the path to wealth. Many others remain unfocused and live life wishing that things were different, wanting something better and wondering what to do.

Building long-term wealth takes time, and life happens while we are making plans. As we move through the various stages of our lives, from entering adulthood, to getting our first job, to getting married and starting a family, through to the empty-nest and retirement stage, our money forms the bedrock upon which we build our lives. It buys us a lifestyle and gives us access to wonderful and enriching experiences. But our money must be made to work for us – we need to balance our enjoyment of today with our needs and goals of tomorrow. I have included a checklist at the end of this chapter so that you can ensure that you have all the financial bases covered.

Getting rich is simple in principle: spend less than you earn, and invest the rest. We have unpacked this in great detail. It is up to you how you use this information to achieve your long-term goals.

You have to make investing a priority. Build a solid portfolio that you keep growing. Equities and property provide sound long-term growth. Money market investments provide liquidity. Other investments provide valuable diversification in times of uncertainty. Appendix 5 summarises all the options we have discussed. Which assets you invest in, and how you access them, is your choice. But, armed with knowledge, you will have empowered yourself to make the right decisions.

We are all different. Some of us enjoy the thrill of investing directly, others want to work with a professional and have them do the work. Some of us take more risks than others, some of us are more eager to learn about investing than others. But, whatever our differences, we all want to build wealth. Let's not ignore the critical area of protecting our wealth as we are building it – the role of life, disability and illness cover.

The smart thing to do is to take the time to understand yourself, and to understand what makes money (and what wastes money), and then to put a plan in place to achieve your goals. You will find the right investment option for you, but, whatever you decide to do, never forget these three golden rules:
1. invest for the long term
2. in an inflation-beating investment
3. with a reputable company or investment that will not disappear overnight.

If you follow these rules, you will not go wrong. One day, in the not-too-distant future, you will look back in awe on what you have achieved. Building wealth and getting rich is within everyone's grasp.

This Smartwoman journey is all about knowledge. The world of money is complicated, but it is also not that difficult if you arm yourself with knowledge. Reading and learning is crucial – curiosity gives us the edge. But knowledge without action is useless if you are aiming to build long-term wealth. Knowledge gives you the platform; you need to take action to achieve meaningful results.

And, as we focus on our money, let's never forget that we are all whole but interconnected people – we are part of society, part of families and communities – and that there are many different aspects to wealth, not just the financial one.

I want to leave you with this final list of thoughts – my Smartwoman Lucky 13 List. If you follow these guidelines, I believe you will be pretty successful at building your wealth and getting rich in all aspects of your life.

The Smartwoman Lucky 13 List

1. Listen more, speak less.
2. Live within your means.
3. Make investment a priority.
4. Give back to others through tithing or charity.
5. Be positive and surround yourself with positive people.
6. Stop self-limiting beliefs.
7. Find joy in living your designer life, not in buying designer stuff.
8. Be curious and have a thirst for learning.
9. Set realistic goals.
10. Go the extra mile and never give up.
11. Network and build strong relationships.
12. Invest in what you understand.
13. Don't gamble or waste your money.

I have done my part and shared what I know. It is now up to you to ring in the changes in your life, take action and get going on your path to wealth. They say that there is no force equal to that of a determined woman. I wish you well on your journey.

YOUR MONEYSMART CHECKLIST

Use this handy checklist to make sure that you have your future on track. Which of the following do you have in place? Tick the boxes and put a plan in place to fill any gaps.

1. An emergency fund	
2. Medical aid cover	
3. Short-term savings fund for specific goals	
4. Longer-term investments for long-term goals	
5. Income protection in case of illness, disability or retrenchment	
6. Life cover with updated beneficiaries	
7. A valid will	
8. A retirement plan	
9. Short-term insurance for your car, home and possessions	

Appendix 1

Appendix 2

Local Market 5 Year Asset Class Returns — March 2021

	2008	2009	2010	2011	2012	2013	2014	2015	2016	2017	2018	2019	5 Yrs*
Best	SA Real Estate 26.88	SA Real Estate 21.57	SA Real Estate 18.06	SA Real Estate 14.25	SA Real Estate 15.89	SA Equity 19.93	SA Real Estate 21.37	Global Equities 27.58	Global Equities 22.08	Global Equities 20.40	Global Equities 11.41	Global Equities 12.94	Global Equities 14.55
	SA Equity 19.01	SA Equity 20.25	SA Equity 15.23	Global Bonds 9.39	SA Bonds 10.84	SA Real Estate 18.86	Global Equities 20.82	Global Bonds 19.62	SA Real Estate 17.29	SA Real Estate 13.86	SA Bonds 7.71	SA Bonds 7.75	SA Bonds 8.67
	SA-MA-High Eq 15.43	SA-MA-High Eq 13.05	SA-MA-High Eq 10.28	SA Bonds 8.60	Global Bonds 10.10	Global Equities 17.93	SA Equity 15.79	SA Real Estate 17.02	SA Equity 12.97	SA Equity 11.93	Global Bonds 7.70	SA Cash 7.19	SA Equity 8.04
	Global Bonds 12.08	Global Bonds 10.31	SA Cash 8.89	SA Cash 8.55	SA Equity 9.41	SA-MA-High Eq 13.08	Global Bonds 12.35	SA Equity 12.96	Global Bonds 11.35	SA-MA-High Eq 9.16	SA Cash 6.91	Global Bonds 6.28	SA Cash 6.75
	SA-MA-Low Eq 10.74	SA-MA-Low Eq 10.03	SA-MA-Low Eq 8.61	SA Equity 8.09	SA-MA-Low Eq 8.12	SA-MA-Low Eq 10.14	SA-MA-High Eq 11.99	SA-MA-High Eq 11.23	SA-MA-High Eq 10.39	Global Bonds 8.70	SA Equity 5.77	SA Equity 5.99	SA-MA-Low Eq 5.93
	SA Bonds 10.42	SA Cash 8.93	SA Bonds 7.91	SA-MA-Low Eq 7.39	SA Cash 7.78	SA Bonds 7.65	SA Bonds 9.97	SA-MA-Low Eq 9.45	SA-MA-Low Eq 8.88	SA-MA-Low Eq 7.08	SA Real Estate 5.70	SA-MA-Low Eq 5.84	SA-MA-High Eq 5.87
	SA Cash 8.70	Global Equities 7.62	Global Bonds 7.57	SA CPI 6.83	SA-MA-High Eq 7.52	Global Bonds 6.54	SA-MA-Low Eq 9.80	SA Bonds 8.09	SA Bonds 7.34	SA Cash 6.50	SA CPI 5.44	SA CPI 4.08	SA CPI 4.38
	SA CPI 6.50	SA Bonds 7.12	SA CPI 6.74	SA-MA-High Eq 6.78	SA CPI 6.25	SA Cash 6.49	SA Cash 5.88	SA Cash 5.77	SA Cash 6.10	SA Bonds 8.27	SA-MA-High Eq 4.83	SA-MA-High Eq 4.83	Global Bonds 3.11
Worst	Global Equities 8.19	SA CPI 6.65	Global Equities 3.30	Global Equities 0.31	Global Equities 3.19	SA CPI 5.00	SA CPI 5.25	SA CPI 5.49	SA CPI 5.62	SA CPI 5.45	SA-MA-High Eq 4.83	SA Real Estate 1.21	SA Real Estate -7.37

All returns are Rand denominated. Performance as at March 2021 | Proxies for Diversified Portfolios: (ASISA) South African - MA - High Equity | (ASISA) South African - MA - Low Equity
*5 Years to March 2021

Source: Morningstar Direct

Appendix 3

Global Market 5 Year Asset Class Returns — March 2021

Sanlam Investments

	2008	2009	2010	2011	2012	2013	2014	2015	2016	2017	2018	2019	5 Yrs*
Best	Emerging Markets Equities 7.66	Emerging Markets Equities 15.51	Emerging Markets Equities 12.78	Global Bonds 6.46	Global Bonds 5.44	North American Equities 17.09	North American Equities 13.60	USD-ZAR Exchange Rate 18.49	North American Equities 12.07	North American Equities 14.15	North American Equities 10.49	North American Equities 14.79	North American Equities 15.74
	USD-ZAR Exchange Rate 7.55	USD-ZAR Exchange Rate 5.60	Global Bonds 6.66	USD-ZAR Exchange Rate 2.96	USD-ZAR Exchange Rate 4.28	Global Property 16.06	Global Property 12.03	North American Equities 10.51	USD-ZAR Exchange Rate 11.15	World Equities 11.64	World Equities 8.74	Emerging Markets Equities 12.81	World Equities 13.30
	Global Bonds 5.01	European Equities 4.74	European Equities 2.98	Emerging Markets Equities 2.41	Global Property 1.07	World Equities 15.02	World Equities 10.20	Global Property 7.96	World Equities 10.41	European Equities 8.37	Global Property 6.53	World Equities 12.19	Emerging Markets Equities 12.07
	European Equities 2.95	Global Bonds 4.56	Global Property 2.88	North American Equities -0.43	North American Equities 0.96	Emerging Markets Equities 14.79	USD-ZAR Exchange Rate 9.12	World Equities 7.59	Global Property 10.33	USD-ZAR Exchange Rate 8.07	European Equities 5.82	European Equities 8.18	European Equities 9.49
	Global Property 1.96	World Equities 2.01	World Equities 2.43	World Equities -2.37	Emerging Markets Equities -0.22	European Equities 12.05	European Equities 4.48	European Equities 4.02	European Equities 7.41	Global Property 7.20	Emerging Markets Equities 5.61	Global Bonds 4.79	Global Property 4.85
	World Equities -0.51	Global Property 2.00	North American Equities 2.38	Global Property -5.28	World Equities -1.18	Global Bonds 3.91	Global Bonds 2.65	Global Bonds 0.90	Emerging Markets Equities 1.28	Emerging Markets Equities 4.35	USD-ZAR Exchange Rate 4.14	Global Property 4.72	Global Bonds 2.66
Worst	North American Equities -2.21	North American Equities 0.74	USD-ZAR Exchange Rate 0.04	European Equities -6.23	European Equities -6.50	USD-ZAR Exchange Rate 1.67	Emerging Markets Equities 1.78	Emerging Markets Equities -4.81	Global Bonds 0.21	Global Bonds 0.79	Global Bonds 2.31	USD-ZAR Exchange Rate -0.67	USD-ZAR Exchange Rate 0.51

All returns are USD denominated. Performance as at March 2021 | Balanced: Proxy for a diversified portfolio: 65% MSCI World | 35% Barclays Global Treasury
*5 Years to March 2021

Source: Morningstar Direct

Appendix 4

Personal tax implications: 2020/21 tax year

Sources of income		Interest	Capital gain	Dividends	Notes
Exemptions		First R23 800 for persons under 65 is tax exempt; for persons aged 65 and older, first R34 500 is tax exempt	First R40 000 is tax exempt; there is a R300 000 capital gain exemption in the year of death		
How tax is calculated		Added to investor's income and taxed according to individual's marginal tax rate	Proceeds minus base cost of the asset; taxable portion added to investor's income and taxed according to individual's marginal tax rate	Dividend withholding tax of 20% of the dividend paid directly to SARS; balance paid to investor	
Investment type	Retail Savings Bonds	✓			
	Money market/cash	✓			
	Equities		✓	✓	

APPENDIX 4

Sources of income		Interest	Capital gain	Dividends	Notes
	ETFs	✓	✓	✓	
	Unit trusts	✓	✓	✓	
	REITs	✓	✓		Dividend received is treated as interest received; interest exemption does not apply
	Tax-free savings account				No tax payable on growth or proceeds; penalty of 40% is levied on all contributions exceeding R36 000 per annum or R500 000 over the lifetime of the investor; this is payable over and above the normal income tax payable
	Investment plans and retirement annuities (RAs)				Tax dependent on the legislation with which the investment complies

Appendix 5

Summary of investment options from high risk to low risk

	Risk	Skill/ knowledge required	Accessibility (how expensive?)	Term (short = less than 2 years; medium = 2–5 years; long = 5 years or more)	Potential return	Type of return
Crypto-currencies	Extremely high	Low	Low	Long	Unknown	Growth only
Equities	High	High	Medium	Long	High	Income and growth
Exchange-traded funds (ETFs)	High	Medium	Medium	Long	High	Income and growth
Real estate property trusts (REITs)	High	Medium	Medium	Long	High	Income and growth
Unit trusts	High	Low	Low	Long	High	Income and growth
Diamonds	Medium	High	Medium	Medium to long	Medium to high	Growth only
Investment plans	Medium	Low	Low	Long	High	Growth only
Bonds	Medium	High	Medium	Medium	Medium	Income and growth
Rental property	Medium to low	Medium	Medium to high	Long	Medium	Income and growth

APPENDIX 5

	Risk	Skill/ knowledge required	Accessibility (how expensive?)	Term (short = less than 2 years; medium = 2–5 years; long = 5 years or more)	Potential return	Type of return
RSA Retail Savings Bonds	Low	Low	Low	Medium	Medium	Income and growth
Cash	Low	Low	Low	Short	Low	Income only
Gold	Low	Low	Low	Medium to long	Medium	Growth only
Art, rare furniture, collectibles	Low	High	Medium	Medium to long	High	Growth only

References

Articles and websites

Ackerman, R. (2012). 'Women & investing: why many advisers are missing out', Investment News, 8 April 2012, http://www.investmentnews.com/article/20120408/REG/304089957/women-investing-why-many-advisers-are-missing-out (accessed 21 December 2016)

American Cancer Society. (2014). 'The history of cancer', https://www.cancer.org/cancer/cancer-basics/history-of-cancer.html (accessed 8 September 2021)

Arde, A. (2017). 'Don't fall for complex schemes', *Personal Finance*, 21 January 2017, http://www.iol.co.za/personal-finance/my-money/dont-fall-for-complex-scams-7462528 (accessed 21 January 2017)

Benjamin, C. (2015). 'Stokvels fly as Wealthhub reinvents itself', Timeslive, 7 June 2015, https://www.timeslive.co.za/sunday-times/business/2015-06-07-stokvels-fly-as-wealth-hub-reinvents-itself/ (accessed 4 October 2021)

Bi India Bureau. (2021). 'South Africa's $4 billion in crypto scams has regulators scrambling to bring in new regulations within the next three to six months', https://www.businessinsider.in/cryptocurrency/news/south-africas-4-billion-in-crypto-scams-has-regulators-scrambling-to-bring-in-new-regulations-within-the-next-three-to-six-months/articleshow/84015957.cms (accessed 3 July 2021)

Blackman, A. (2014). 'Can money buy you happiness?', *The Wall Street Journal*, 10 November 2014, http://www.wsj.com/articles/can-money-buy-happiness-heres-what science-has-to-say-1415569538 (accessed 8 December 2016)

BrainyQuote. (n.d.). 'Michelangelo Quotes', https://www.brainyquote.com/quotes/quotes/m/michelange108779.html (accessed 19 December 2016)

———. https://www.brainyquote.com/topics/money-quotes (accessed 9 June 2021)

Brown, M. (2016). 'December 2016 – etfSA.co.za monthly South African ETF, ETN and unit trust passive index tracking performance survey', http://www.etfsa.co.za/docs/perfsurvey/perf_survey_dec2016.pdf (accessed 2 August 2021)

Buffett, W. (2016). 'Warren Buffett's top 10 pieces on investment advice', *Simply Safe Dividends*, 25 July 2016, http://www.simplysafedividends.com/warren-buffett-investment-advice/ (accessed 5 January 2016)

Business Insider SA. (2021). 'SA's online retail has more than doubled in two years – but the best is probably over', https://www.businessinsider.co.za/sas-online-retail-has-more-than-doubled-in-two-years-but-the-best-is-probably-over-2021-5 (accessed 8 June 2021)

BusinessTech. (2016a). 'South African unemployment rate hits 13 year high', 22 November 2016, https://businesstech.co.za/news/government/144055/south-african-unemployment-rate-hits-13-year-high/ (accessed 31 December 2016)

———. (2016b). '8 things to consider before investing in property', 22 December 2016, https://businesstech.co.za/news/wealth/148251/8-things-to-consider-before-investing-in-property/ (accessed 4 January 2017)

Cairns, P. (2013). 'The state of SA's unit trust industry', Moneyweb, 11 March 2013, https://www.moneyweb.co.za/archive/the-state-of-sas-unit-trust-industry/ (accessed 9 February 2017)

———. (2016). 'How to grow your real wealth', Moneyweb, 22 March 2016, http://www.moneyweb.co.za/investing/grow-real-wealth/ (accessed 20 December 2016)

Cameron, J. (2014). 'Five great reasons to invest in unit trusts', BizNews.com, 14 April 2014 (no longer available online).

Cape Gold Coin Exchange. (n.d.). 'Krugerrand prices over the years', http://www.krugerrandsa.co.za/index.php/history/prices (accessed 1 June 2021)

Cars.co.za. (2013). 'How car depreciation affects the value of a car', 3 June 2013, http://www.cars.co.za/motoring_news/car_info/how_car_depreciation_affects_the_valu_of_a_car/#.WPCO-lKB3ok (accessed 30 December 2016)

Chetty, I. (2021). 'Over 30% of South Africans have a side hustle', https://ventureburn.com/2021/03/over-30-of-south-africans-have-a-side-hustle/ (accessed 15 June 2021)

REFERENCES

City Press. (2015). 'The ABC of investing via ETFs', News24, 2 March 2015, http://www.news24.com/Archives/City-Press/The-ABC-of-investing-via-ETFs-20150429 (accessed 11 January 2017)

Crotty, A. (2017). 'Tribunal ruling may cost Edcon millions'; *Business Day*, 3 May 2017 https://www.businesslive.co.za/bd/companies/retail-and-consumer/2017-05-03-tribunal-finds-the-club-fee-charged-by-edcon-to-be-unlawful/ (accessed 2 August 2021)

Davila, D. (2016). '9 questions you should ask before hiring a robo-adviser', Money, 23 September 2016, https://time.com/4505053/9-questions-you-should-ask-before-hiring-a-robo-adviser/ (accessed 29 September 2021)

Dolan, K., J. Wang, C. Peteren-Withorn (editors). (2021). 'Forbes world billionaires list 2021', https://www.forbes.com/billionaires/ (accessed 7 June 2021)

Du Preez, L. (2016a). 'Enter the robo-financial adviser', Personal Finance, 10 March 2016, http://www.iol.co.za/personal-finance/financial-planning/enter-the-robo-financial-adviser-1996263 (accessed 29 December 2016)

———. (2016b). 'Dealing with the financial fall-out of divorce', Personal Finance, 13 December 2016, http://www.iol.co.za/personal-finance/dealing-with-the-financial-fall-out-of-divorce-7171204 (accessed 29 December 2016)

Ferentchak, L. (2016). 'Why smart clients do dumb things', *Proactive Advisor Magazine*, 3 March 2016, http://proactiveadvisormagazine.com/poor-investing-decisions/ (accessed 23 December 2016)

Fisher-French, M. (2016). 'Are gold coins a good investment?', Maya on Money, 16 May 2016, http://mayaonmoney.co.za/2016/05/gold-coins-good-investment/ (accessed 9 January 2017)

Gerencer, B. (2021). 'Black collar crime: Pastor Colin Davids accused of running a Ponzi scheme', https://brucegerencser.net/2017/04/black-collar-crime-pastor-colin-davids-accused-running-ponzi-scheme/ (accessed 17 June 2021)

Girlboss, '10 Money Quotes by Women That'll Inspire You to Make Some', https://www.girlboss.com/read/money-quotes-women (accessed 6 July 2021)

Government Employees Pension Fund (GEPF), www.gepf.gov.za (accessed 19 December 2016)

Greeka.com. (n.d.). 'King Midas and his touch', http://www.greeka.com/greece myths/king-midas.htm (accessed 19 December 2016)

Holland, K. (2015). 'Fighting with your spouse? It's probably about this', CNBC, 4 February 2015, http://www.cnbc.com/2015/02/04/money-is-the-leading-cause-of-stress-in relationships.html (accessed 16 December 2016)

HYIP.com. (n.d.). 'The Kubus scheme: The greatest scam of the 80s', http://hyip.com/2016/06/21/greatest-scam-80s/ (accessed 11 November 2016)

Investment Funds Institute of Canada. (n.d.). 'Value of advice', https://www.ific.ca/en/policy_topics/value-of-advice (accessed 31 December 2016)

Jasen, G. (2015). 'Male investors vs. female investors', *The Wall Street Journal*, 3 May 2015, https://www.wsj.com/articles/male-investors-vs-female-investors-how-do-they-compare-1430709406 (accessed 21 December 2016)

JSE. (n.d.). 'Government Bonds', https://www.jse.co.za/trade/debt-market/bonds/government bonds (accessed 5 January 2017)

Knoema.com. (2021). 'South Africa – life expectancy at age 60 for both sexes combined', https://knoema.com/atlas/South-Africa/topics/Demographics/Age/Life-expectancy-at-age-60-years (accessed 16 June 2021)

Mesch, D. (2016). 'The gender gap in charitable giving', *The Wall Street Journal*, 1 February 2016, http://www.wsj.com/articles/the-gender-gap-in-charitable-giving-1454295689 (accessed 21 December 2016)

Mahlangu, I. (2014). 'Lotto win changes lives, but not always for the better', Timeslive, 29 November 2014, https://www.timeslive.co.za/sunday-times/lifestyle/2014-11-29-lotto-win-changes-lives-but-not-always-for-the-better/ (accessed 4 October 2021)

MindTools. (n.d.). 'Personal goal setting', https://www.mindtools.com/page6.html (accessed 19 December 2016)

Mngadi, Z., and M. Parkin. (2001). 'Miracle 2000 mastermind admits his guilt', IOL News, 28 June 2001, http://www.iol.co.za/news/south-africa/miracle-2000-mastermind-admits-his-guilt 68795 (accessed 11 November 2016)

Moodley, N. (2015). 'The fine art of investing in art', Fin24, 26 July 2015, http://www.fin24.com/Money/Investments/The-fine-art-of-investing-in-art-20150725 (accessed 9 January 2017)

Nordqvist, C. (2014). 'What is neuroscience?', Medical News Today, 26 September 2014, http://www.medicalnewstoday.com/articles/248680.php (accessed 30 November 2016)

REFERENCES

NPR 50. (2008). 'Understanding the science of shopping', https://www.npr.org/templates/story/story.php?storyId=98184836 (accessed 8 June 2020)

Ohio State University Research News. (2005). 'Divorce drops a person's wealth by 77 percent, study finds', Ohio State University, https://news.osu.edu/divorce-drops-a-persons-wealth-by-77-percent-study-finds/ (accessed 20 December 2016)

Old Mutual Savings and Investment Monitor. (2019). https://www.oldmutual.co.za/savingsmonitor/ (accessed 16 August 2021)

Rateweb.co.za. (2020). 'How to choose a financial adviser in South Africa', 23 December 2020, https://www.rateweb.co.za/news/how-to-choose-a-financial-advisor-in-south-africa/ (accessed 2 July 2021)

Rosenberg, E. (2021). 'Robo-advisors vs. financial advisors', Investor Junkie, 19 April 2021, https://investorjunkie.com/robo-advisors/robo-advisors-vs-financial-advisors/ (accessed 4 October 2021)

Royal Geographical Society. (n.d.). 'Who wants to live forever?', https://www.rgs.org/schools/teaching-resources/who-wants-to-live-forever/why-are-people-living-longer/ (accessed 31 December 2016)

Royal, J., and K. Voigt. (2021). 'What is cryptocurrency? Here's what you should know', https://www.nerdwallet.com/article/investing/cryptocurrency-7-things-to-know (accessed 3 July 2021)

Sandhurst Trustees. (n.d.). 'Income vs growth' (no longer available online)

Sanlam Benchmark Survey. (2016). 'Rethinking retirement through a new dimension', https://www.sanlam.co.za/corporate/retirement/benchmarksurvey/Documents/Pensioner%20Databook/Pensioner-Databook-2016.pdf (accessed 10 January 2017)

Search Quotes. (n.d.). Money vs relationship quotes, http://www.searchquotes.com/search/Money_Vs_Relationship/ (accessed 16 December 2016)

Shimansky, Y. (2016). 'Why investing in diamonds is not for the faint-hearted', Cover, 12 February 2016, https://www.cover.co.za/why-investing-in-diamonds-is-not-for-the-faint-hearted/ (accessed 9 January 2017)

Smillie, S. (2017). 'MMM's Bitcoin comeback', Business Report, 28 January 2017, http://www.iol.co.za/business-report/technology/mmms-bitcoin-comeback-7541944 (accessed 28 January 2017)

South African REIT Association. (n.d.). http://www.sareit.com

South African Savings Institute. (n.d.). https://savingsinstitute.co.za/resources/overview-of-asset-classes/ (accessed 4 October 2021)

Statistics South Africa. (2019). 'How unequal is South Africa', http://www.statssa.gov.za/?p=12930 (accessed 15 May 2021)

Story, C., and K. Cherney. (2016). 'The history of heart disease', Healthline, 12 February 2016, http://www.healthline.com/health/heart-disease/history (accessed 31 December 2016)

Tarrant, H. (2016). 'South African robo-advisers, compared', Moneyweb, 22 August 2016, http://www.moneyweb.co.za/investing/south-african-robo-advisors-compared/ (accessed 30 December 2016)

The Corporate Sister. (2021). 'Quotes about money from famous women that will make you financially savvy', https://www.thecorporatesister.com/blog/12-quotes-about-money-from-famous-women-thatll-make-you-financially-savvy (accessed 6 July 2021)

The Economist. (2000). 'South Africa's collapsing pyramids', 3 August 2000, https://www.economist.com/international/2000/08/03/south-africas-collapsing-pyramids (accessed 23 September 2021)

The Guardian. (2013). 'Vitamin supplements are a waste of money, say scientists', 17 December 2013, https://www.theguardian.com/lifeandstyle/2013/dec/17/vitamin-supplements-waste-money-scientists (accessed 16 December 2016)

The New Message from God. (2008). 'Building the four pillars of your life', http://www.newmessage.org/the-message/other-revelations/building-the-four-pillars-of-your-life (accessed 10 December 2016)

Van den Berg, S. (2015). 'Influence: rand-cost averaging can protect the value of your money', Accountancy South Africa, 16 September 2015, http://www.accountancysa.org.za/influence-rand-cost-averaging-can-protect-the-value-of-your-money/ (accessed 20 December 2016)

Western Cape Government. (2015). 'What you need to know about marriage contracts', https://www.westerncape.gov.za/general-publication/what-you-need-know-about-marriage-contracts (accessed 16 August 2021).

Zwane, T. (2020). 'The gender pay gap keeps widening in South Africa', *City Press*, 9 August 2020, https://www.news24.com/citypress/business/the-gender-pay-gap-keeps-widening-in-south-africa-20200809 (accessed 7 June 2021)

Books

Alvesson, M., and A. Spicer. (2015). *The Stupidity Paradox*. London: Profile Books

Kahneman, D. (2011). *Thinking, Fast and Slow*. New York: Farrar, Straus and Giroux

Koh, L. (2008). *Your Money Personality: Unlock the Secret to a Rich and Happy Life*. Wellington, NZ: Awa Press

Larter, R. (2017) *How to Make Money on the Stock Exchange*. Cape Town: Penguin Random House

Lewis, D. (2013). *The Brain Sell: When Science Meets Shopping*. London: Quercus

Preller, B. (2013). *Everyone's Guide to Divorce and Separation*. Cape Town: Random House Struik

Stanovich, K.E. (2010). *Decision Making and Rationality in the Modern World*. New York: Oxford University Press

Underhill, P. (2008). *Why We Buy: The Science of Shopping*. New York: Simon & Schuster